MW00488549

ART OF TEA

ART OF TEA

A JOURNEY OF RITUAL, DISCOVERY, AND IMPACT

STEVE SCHWARTZ

LIONCREST
PUBLISHING

Hardcover ISBN: 978-1-5445-2778-9
Paperback ISBN: 978-1-5445-2776-5
eBook ISBN: 978-1-5445-2777-2
Audiobook ISBN: 978-1-5445-2779-6

To my wife and kids for filling my cup in meaningful ways.

CONTENTS

INTRODUCTION

I believe that each of us is driven by something. Each of us has that thing that acts as rocket fuel to propel us forward and provide the potential to allow us to soar to greater heights.

My rocket fuel comes from the notion of *impact*.

Even as the founder of Art of Tea, it's not the tea I formulate and blend that I expect to impact the world in and of itself. (Although, as I will explain in these pages, I firmly believe that tea *can* have a significant impact on our physical, mental, and emotional wellness.) It's the place tea holds in our lives that I see as impactful. In a rapidly moving world, tea is timeless, and it's analog. It offers us a simple way to incorporate sensory experience and ritual into our daily lives in the modern world.

I believe deeply in the importance of ritual in our daily lives, even if it's just a few moments a day. I believe that if more people figure out how to incorporate their own rituals on a regular basis, the entire world can change for the better. In these pages, I'm going to explain why that's important and what it can look like.

It's no mistake that rituals have been around for about as long as human beings have. Ritual gives us the opportunity to tune into and connect with ourselves, with others, and with the world around us. Depending upon your belief system, ritual might even provide an inroad for connecting with something greater than yourself. It's for *this* reason that I believe not only in the power of drinking tea but also in the power of the small acts necessary to prepare and serve the tea. In the moments you are preparing, serving, and drinking your tea, it may seem like a small thing. But compounded over time, building this ritual into your routine can have a significant impact on your life. I know it has on mine.

In case you haven't guessed already, I view tea as sacred. Yes, part of the appeal of tea is that it's good for us from a physical health and wellness perspective. But I also believe tea impacts us on an energetic level, and the production and distribution of tea influences that impact long before you begin the tea ritual in your home. In my mind, it's critical that the ingredients that go into each batch of tea are harvested in a beautiful, sacred space where they can soak in the sun, earth, and rain. They should be produced mindfully and picked with care. It's for this reason that we're so serious about sourcing the herbs and botanicals in our tea and go to such great lengths to source the best of the best, no matter how far off of the beaten track that hunt takes us. It's also why the production process at Art of Tea is so intentional—in fact, we consider that sacred too. We believe that how we treat our tea matters. We believe that the energy we put into our tea makes an impact on the people who drink it—even if that impact is subtle.

In the past eighteen years, I've seen firsthand how more and more people are excited about and intrigued by tea. Yes, this is good for business, but that shift makes me happy for so many reasons that extend beyond the bottom line. Tea makes us better on just about every level: it heals us, it sharpens our focus, it balances our nervous system—and that's just the beginning.

Once upon a time, the world was broken up into two distinct populations: tea drinkers and coffee drinkers. There was no crossing the line and going over to the dark side, regardless of which side was dark, depending upon your stance. Today, all of that has changed. Many people drink both coffee and tea (just like many people drink both beer and wine), and most associate certain times of day with one drink or the other. In fact, people create rituals around those times, even though they may not think of it like that.

Tea used to be a drink for your grandma or for British people. According to the Tea Association of America, 87 percent of millennials drink tea. Not only that, but tea is the second-most consumed beverage in the world, second only to water. This next one surprises a lot of people, but it's true: more men than women drink tea. Once upon a time, tea wasn't considered manly, but as we've become more educated and aware of health and wellness in our daily lives, that's changed too.

About fifteen years ago, when coffee was all the rage and tea was just a drink to tolerate when you had the flu, I had the sense that tea hadn't yet had its moment—but it was coming. When I started peddling tea, I was asked more than once, "What are you doing?" "You should get into coffee," well-intentioned friends advised me. Thankfully, I didn't listen.

I'm sure you won't be surprised to hear that, for as much as I anticipated the current tea trend in America, tea was around long before I was. Five thousand years before me, to be exact. So, while the trend of tea-drinking might be relatively recent in mainstream America, it's a timeless beverage with ancient roots. We'll get into all of this soon.

Tea and ritual aren't the only things that have impacted me, nor are they the only things I want to share. Life is much more nuanced than that. As I look back on my own life, I can see the ways in which I have been shaped and given direction by the various people, places, and events I've encountered. I am the person I am, walking the path I am walking as a direct result. While I might not have chosen some of the events in my life if given the choice—such as being pushed out into the world and left to my own devices at thirteen and losing my mother to a terminal illness at eighteen—all of it had a role in making me who I am today. Even as I write this book in the midst of the COVID-19 crisis, I'm constantly reminded of how even challenging times can impact us in positive ways. These are the times in life that force us to grow, to evolve, to reevaluate, to become more.

In this book, I'll share some of my own journey and how a series of events beyond my control ultimately led me down a path I might have never chosen otherwise. That path has included the guidance of Ayurvedic masters, out-of-the way herbal apothecaries in Israel, majestic tea fields in Asia, and building a business that allows me to interact and grow with like-minded people who believe in what we're bringing into the world just as much as I do.

I'm excited to share much of what I've been so lucky to learn over the years with you. I'm hopeful that this information will inspire you to bring the benefits of tea—in particular, the ritualistic aspect of tea—into your own life and home. And, most of all, I hope that these things will impact your life for the better, just as they have mine.

PART ONE

MY STORY

CHAPTER ONE

WELCOME TO ADULTHOOD

The first twelve years of my life were what I now understand to be very fortunate. I grew up as the youngest of three children in Westlake Village, California, which was like a kid's version of paradise. Every day after school, me and my crew rode our bikes all over the place until it was time to come home for dinner. I went to private school, my family had a live-in housekeeper, and vacations sometimes involved limos and Hawaii. There was never a sense of scarcity or lack. That was my normal.

Fortunately normal, as I would come to realize.

When I was twelve years old, my dad sent me to survival camp in Northern California. I left Westlake Village as a chunky, dorky, spoiled kid and found myself roughing it for six weeks with a fifty-five-pound backpack strapped on my back. All of the other kids there were in a very different position than I was: for them, it was either juvenile hall or survival camp. Survival camp seemed like the better option. I'm sure you can imagine how being in this sort of environment was a shock to my system.

At one point in that six-week period, everyone started arguing. Fed up, I'm sure, the leader stopped us all in the middle of the wilderness and said, "Okay, guys, we need a leader." In response, everyone pointed to me, which was shocking, because I was the youngest of all the boys in the group. Looking back, I can see that despite my young age, I had the ability to sift through the noise and make clear decisions.

Survival camp was also my first introduction to meditation. I noticed that the counselors often sat around with their eyes closed for extended periods of time. When I asked them what they were doing, they explained that they were meditating. I had no idea what that was or what it entailed, but they told me that all I had to do was go sit on a rock by the river a little bit upstream from camp, close my eyes, and focus on my breath.

"Well, I can do that," I thought. So I did. At the time, I had no idea that what I was learning in that moment would carry me on for many, many years to come. I remember the feeling of an omnipresent sensation of nature all around me. Time took on a different meaning. The sounds of the river next me and the flow of breath coming in and out of my lungs filled me with a new presence of being . This practice of breathing I learned I can take with me anywhere in the most trying situations as a powerful tool I continuously try to reinforce daily.

Right around that same time, my parents got divorced. Their divorce was a nasty one, and both of them lost everything in the process. Neither of them wanted the courts to think they had money, so both of them refused to financially support us kids. Basically, we were used as bait for money, and as the youngest, I was the primary pawn. My sister had already moved to Tucson, Arizona, for college, and very quickly, my brother followed.

Suddenly, life looked much different than it ever had before. At the age of thirteen, when all of my Jewish friends were celebrating their bar mitzvahs, I decided to skip mine. The divorce was just too ugly to involve both of my parents at a single event, and I was also aware that bar mitzvahs were expensive. I lived with my dad and his new wife for about six months, and then I was sent to a boarding school in Montecito, California, until eighth-grade graduation. Shortly after that, my father's wife dropped me off at the airport, telling me I was going to visit my brother Dave in Tucson for the summer.

That "summer" ended up lasting for the next four years.

Of course, I had my older brother with me, but for all intents and purposes, I was left to my own devices from that point forward. Dave and I weren't very close to begin with, and after all, he was only a teenager himself. So, there I found myself on my own in a place I didn't know. I was a young kid from a sheltered upbringing with no resources and without a lot of survival mechanisms. After a few months of subsisting on margarine and bread, I called my dad to ask if he could send me some money.

"Do you live in a neighborhood?" he asked in response.

"Yes," I replied, confused.

"Are there houses in the neighborhood?" he asked.

"Yes," I said again.

"Do those houses have windows?"

"Yes."

"Then go knock on their doors and see if you can clean them."

I was stunned and more than a little bit freaked out. As a kid who grew up with a housekeeper, cleaning sounded challenging. Let alone *having* to clean in order to survive. But the fact remained that I had to eat. With no other alternative, I picked a house in the neighborhood, took a deep breath, and knocked on the door. A really cute girl who appeared to be about my age answered. My cheeks burned as I asked her if I could clean her family's house or do anything else to help out. My cheeks burned even hotter when she said no.

I kept knocking on doors because I had to, until eventually, an older couple agreed to let me clean their house. Let me tell you, I butchered the job, but they were very kind and continued to employ me. Over time, I got better at cleaning, and more people agreed to hire me on to help out around their houses. After a while, I figured out how to landscape too. In the process of all of this, I learned a lot about tenacity and the power of trial and error. Due to nothing other than sheer will and desperation, I managed to get by.

Thankfully, I was a towering six four by the time I reached my early teens, which made it easy enough for me to lie about my age. This came in handy for someone in a situation like mine. I was able to supplement my housecleaning and landscaping gigs with a job at Arby's before I was of legal age. I quickly learned that if you want to keep your job at Arby's—which I definitely *did* want to do—it's necessary to become adept at customer service. The rule at this Arby's location was that if a customer tells a manager that an employee needs to be fired, that employee gets fired, no questions asked. I decided then that if I were to start a company I would flip the priorities so that we would be a people first organization.

I managed to make ends meet throughout my high school career simply because I was willing to do whatever it took. But there were still days when I had no money when the $1.50 it cost to buy lunch at school was more than I could afford. On those days, I had to wait it out to see if one of my friends had leftovers they were willing to pass my way. My friends knew about my situation, although, of course as kids, they didn't fully understand it.

In many ways, life continued to get more and more difficult as my teenage years went on and my responsibilities mounted. My saving grace was that I made a concerted effort to see everything as an adventure, even if that adventure consisted of walking home from school in 120-degree heat. I was able to find little spots of joy, even in moments of pain. For whatever reason, I also had an incredible sense of foresight. Even as a teenager, I remember thinking about the fact that the decisions I made in any given moment would be decisions that I would recall later in life. I framed my young life and the choices I made by thinking about the lessons I would want to share with my own kids when I got older. Looking back, I suspect this was my way of attempting to find purpose in my life and circumstances.

At the same time, I also felt confused, abandoned, and alone. I latched on to the few friends I had as a teenager, and it hurt me deeply when those relationships didn't work out. My friends and their parents were puzzled by my situation. "I don't get it," they would say. "*Where* are your parents?" Sometimes I had to lie when it came to things like getting a parent's signature for something at school, and I knew for a fact there was no chance either of them would show up for anything parents were supposed to attend. Although I accepted my circumstances, I still felt deep pain about my situation. It's a pain that occasionally rears its head to this day, now that I have a fourteen-year-old daughter of my own. I sometimes wonder how I'm supposed to know how to parent a teenager when I was never parented as a teenager myself.

On occasion, I would call my mom collect from a pay phone. When I was fifteen, on one of those calls, my mom told me that she thought I would enjoy being a camp counselor at a Jewish summer camp. I was nervous about the idea at first because I hadn't set foot in camp since survival camp a few years before. Not to mention the fact that I wasn't old enough—camp counselors had to be sixteen. My mom reminded me of what I had already learned through Arby's: that I had adapted to my situation this far and could keep stretching and evolving with new situations. I could make things happen. My mom's confidence that I could pull off being a counselor gave me confidence in myself. And it turns out she was right—I *could* do it. My role as a camp counselor was one of the biggest ways in which I found purpose and joy during those teenage years. In the end, being a counselor armed me with a whole lot more confidence.

Camp afforded me an environment in which I could feel free to be dorky and shine in that capacity. In addition to being a counselor, I was also the theater and outdoor director. I wanted to do everything. Most of all, I loved helping kids who were younger than me and offering the type of guidance I wished I had in my own life. Camp felt like freedom and relief to me. Knowing where my next meal was coming from and that room and board were taken care of was a big deal for a kid in my situation. Once I started working as a counselor, I found myself holding my breath for nine months out of the year, waiting until the time when I could go back to camp and feel like part of something bigger.

Because it was a Jewish camp, being there also made me feel connected to my tribe. In Tucson, there weren't many Jewish people. In fact, there was only one other Jewish kid in my entire high school. It was at camp that I finally had my bar mitzvah at age seventeen. A rabbi there found out that I had skipped mine at the traditional age of thirteen and decided it was time. Three weeks later, the ceremony was held at camp. It was beautiful out there in nature and a rare occasion, because I invited my mom, sister, and a few close friends, and they came to share the moment with me. I appreciated the ritual of becoming a man; it felt like an important rite of passage.

Once I finished high school, I moved out of my brother's house and into my own place with a few of my friends. It was a blast. We frequently went out to the desert and organized elaborate electronic festivals, often going so far as to bring in musical artists from Chicago, New York, and all over the place. This was my first taste of starting a business with a little money, creating a lot of marketing buzz, selling tickets, and figuring out how to pay for top talent. I also loved the feeling of having everyone gathered together and moving to a single beat. It felt like being surrounded by a tribal community. Finally, it seemed as if I had achieved freedom and was living a life that looked and felt the way I wanted it to.

Then came the news that my mom had been diagnosed with breast cancer.

It was jarring news, but the doctors predicted she would recover, and we believed them. Of course we did. Then one day, my mom realized that her arm was reaching for a cup, even though she didn't remember making that movement. It was a strange experience, so she told her doctor about it and asked what he made of the whole thing.

"It's fine," he told her. "Just a symptom of chemo."

That answer didn't land right with my mom, though, so she insisted on having an MRI. It was then that they discovered a grapefruit-sized tumor in her brain.

My mom needed help, and at that point, I was the only viable option. My brother and mom weren't close, and my sister was hard at work getting her doctorate in psychology. I returned to California, not without animosity. Here I was, taking care of someone who had not taken care of me. My mom knew it was a shitty, unfair situation too. She felt bad about my high school years and owned the fact that she hadn't been there for me.

I spent the next ten months caring for my mom in her final days. As the weeks passed by, this included everything from feeding her to cleaning up after her when she went to the bathroom. All cancer is horrible, but brain cancer wreaks a specific type of deterioration as it takes over and alters the body's central operating system. After a while, my mom couldn't walk, but she didn't remember that fact when she woke up in the middle of the night, so she would fall out of bed, and I would have to come rescue her. After this happened a few times, I started staying awake all night long so that I could prevent scenarios like this from unfolding.

Several years after my mother died, I realized exactly how addicted to stress and vigilance I had become during those ten months. A roommate told me that I literally slept with my eyes open. She didn't realize that something was off until she shared feedback with me the following morning. It was only then that I consciously understood I had become so addicted to stress that I never shut down; in some way, I was always on. Of course, stress exists for a reason—it kept us alive during the cavemen days. However, we're no longer living in caves, and still so many of us live in a constant state of survival mode.

While I wasn't aware of the grave toll this stress was taking on me at the time, to some degree, I did understand that I needed to find some sort of release valve. One night, as I was feeling generally overwhelmed like I often did during that period of time I was caring for my mom, I watched a documentary. As I laid there on the couch feeling sorry for myself, a man in his seventies came onscreen and started explaining how yoga had changed his life in both physically and emotionally profound ways. The way in which he spoke of his experience reeked of authenticity, and I wanted some of what he was talking about for myself.

Back then, in the mid-nineties, there wasn't a yoga studio on every corner like there is today, so I was lucky that I was in LA, where there was some presence. After that night on the couch, I started taking yoga classes on a regular basis. Each time, class felt like a retreat. Yoga allowed me to step back from my own life a bit and to watch the processes that were happening within me unfold without labeling or judging them. In certain moments, the practice of yoga felt like the physical manifestation of my emotional experience of life during that time. I would reach a point of pain in a posture at which I didn't think I could hold myself up against gravity any longer. Once I broke through that moment, though, I felt weightless and light, almost as if I were flying. Because that was possible in yoga, I believed it could be possible in other areas of life as well.

As I continued practicing over the years, yoga has helped me feel and understand the difference between bad stress and good stress. The hypervigilance I fell into during those final months of my mom's life was unhealthy, but I understood that there was also a good kind of stress that could build up the type of productive energy that motivates and propels a person forward. Yoga transformed me physically, mentally, and emotionally. It continues to do so to this day.

Yoga also helped me understand I was part of something bigger than myself and that particular moment in my life. One evening, we all sat around the studio in a huge circle and started chanting *om* together. After a while, I could feel the reverberation of my voice with other people's voices. There was an incredibly powerful, almost euphoric sense of connectivity in the room. At the end of class, the teacher said, "How you feel right now—that tingle, the energy, the cellular vibrancy—you feel that all of the time. It's just that, usually, you're too busy to recognize it." I wanted more of *that*. I wanted to tap into that energy, and I wanted to figure out how to access it off the mat too.

At one point during those final weeks, my mom, sister, and I went on a trip to San Francisco. One day, when it was just my mom and me in our hotel room, she turned to me and asked, "Do you have any questions for me? I will tell you anything and be completely transparent."

It was an amazing moment of connection as the two of us sat in that room together on what we both knew would be my mom's last vacation. It's funny because, today, I don't remember what I asked her or what she said. What mattered and what continues to matter to this day is that we had that moment together with all of the walls down between us.

When Mom was in a coma, and it was clear the end was near, we called Dave and told him it was time to come home to say goodbye. When Dave arrived, he, my sister, and I held hands and formed a circle around our mother's bed.

"It's okay, Mom," my sister said. "Dave's here. You can go now."

As soon as my sister said the words, my mom inhaled deeply and exhaled in a long sigh, which seemed to be her way of acknowledging and responding to what had been said. A few minutes later, Mom passed.

It was incredible—life changing, really—to watch as my mom's spirit left her body. Even though her physical body was right there in front of me, it was clear that she was totally gone. I am grateful to have had this experience, which was so difficult but also so beautiful. In our society today, so many of us miss out on this natural part of life. I am deeply appreciative to have been there in that moment, and I walked away with a profoundly greater appreciation of life. Although it was a difficult and challenging time, it was also formative to experience death in this sort of close-up manner at such a young age.

In the wake of my mom's death, I found that there was a vacuum in my life. I had spent all of my time over the past several months caring for her, and now it seemed there was nothing to do except for yoga and swimming. I also felt a sense of urgency. I knew that I had to live life to the fullest and to live it in such a way that my life would be an example to my kids—who didn't even exist at that point.

Even then, I knew I wanted to have an impact.

CHAPTER TWO

FINDING MY PATH

In the wake of my mom's death, I found myself searching. She had followed the path of conventional Western medicine throughout her battle with cancer, and it had failed us. Throughout her battle, my mom and I had spoken to one doctor after another, including leading neurosurgeons and oncology specialists, and even professors. We saw those medical professionals as gods: whatever they believed, we believed. Doctors had told us that various treatments had a high probability of working. Each time, we got our hopes up only to find that the treatments were ineffective. Like most Americans, I had been brought up to believe in the power and efficacy of modern medicine, and yet, clearly, they hadn't worked for us.

I was also struck by the fact that, in retrospect, we all understood that my mom had been sick for a long time before she or anyone else ever realized she had cancer. The fact that a person could have no idea they were as sick as she was confused me. I wondered how many other people were completely unaware of what was happening in their own bodies. It began to dawn on me how disconnected human beings today actually are from themselves, both physically and emotionally. For evidence of this, look no further than how most Americans eat: we don't even take the time to notice whether or not we're full or how certain foods make us feel. We're disconnected from the sensation of how what we take into our bodies impacts us. For instance, I bet you know at least one person who didn't notice for years that they were lactose intolerant. I promise you, there were signs there all along that might have clued them in. Perhaps they felt foggy or a lack of energy after eating cheese but discounted it. Our body is constantly sending us messages; it's just that we often don't pay enough attention to heed them.

Also, I wanted answers. I wanted to figure out how to keep myself and my loved ones healthy so that no one I loved ever had to experience the type of pain that my mom had just gone through.

In the months after my mom died, I had a lot of time to think and reflect. I thought about the fact that cancer must have been around for thousands of years, even if it had only been labeled as cancer in recent times. I became intrigued by alternative modalities. If Western medicine wasn't, in fact, failproof, then what else was out there? I felt driven to unearth solutions we might have missed and started digging into ancient texts to see if I could find some answers there. I spent a lot of time in libraries, bookstores, and metaphysical stores searching for whatever magical solution it was that had eluded us in my mom's final months. I became fixated on cracking the code. More than once, I asked myself what exactly I was doing. After all, I knew I didn't want to be a doctor, a neurologist, an acupuncturist, or a massage therapist. But still, I couldn't stop. I didn't want to.

As I researched, I became deeply intrigued by plant medicine. I was particularly struck by a book written by a gentleman named Dr. Vasant Lad, called *Ayurveda: The Science of Self-Healing*. Before I stumbled across it, I had no idea what Ayurveda was, but the philosophy landed with me, and I quickly came to feel like Ayurveda was everything.

Ayurveda is an ancient medical science from India. Broken down in Sanskrit, Ayurveda literally means the knowledge (*veda*) of life (*ayur*). I came to learn that Ayurveda offers a complete picture of what is happening to an individual in a holistic way, from both an internal and external perspective, as well as how those elements interact. It takes everything into account: how old they are, what they eat, where they live, environmental factors that could be causing stress, and so much more. Only after this investigation has been completed does Ayurveda begin to seek solutions, whether that means preventative care or treatment to resolve an existing issue. Ayurveda understands the body as a connective organism. So often in Western medicine, we never stop to consider that an issue that presents itself in one part of the body might actually originate in a totally different part of the body. Ayurveda seeks to get to the *root* of the problems rather than merely alleviating symptoms. Also, Ayurveda does not present itself as a silver bullet. Instead, it offers a pathway to creating a lifestyle that leads an individual toward the most healthy, vibrant, complete, and intentional life possible. It understands that this lifestyle looks different for every single person. Ayurveda touches upon every facet of life, and that's what I loved most about it when I first discovered it. That's what I continue to love most about Ayurveda to this day.

The application of Ayurveda involved some of the things that resonated with me and that I was already practicing, including yoga and meditation. It also encompassed topics I was increasingly interested in, such as herbology, diet, lifestyle, and ancient healing practices. It even discussed oncology and cardiovascular health and fitness. In addition to all of this, I liked that Ayurveda was based on ancient wisdom and that the depth of the practice offered the opportunity for mentorship and lifelong journey. *All* of that spoke to me. It felt like I had found the mothership, and Dr. Lad was the modern-day captain of that ship. I knew I had to learn more.

I found out that Dr. Lad was the director of the Ayurvedic Institute in Albuquerque, New Mexico. I contacted the school, and it turned out they offered a weekend course on the psychology of Ayurveda. I had to go. I'm so glad I did because, in the course of that weekend, I fell in love with the place.

Dr. Lad was simultaneously delicate and gentle, while also incredibly powerful. He had a glow about him, was always smiling and present, and seemed alive in a way I had never witnessed before. I would go so far as to say that Dr. Lad was the embodiment of the light that comes from true, deep health and wellness. He described himself as an artist by choice and a physician by trade. He was very intentional about everything he did and encouraged us to find the beauty and art in everything we did. Dr. Lad was a simple man, but when he spoke, it was almost as if everyone went into a deep trance state. He had the ability to unpack knowledge in a way that felt as if he was transferring it in the truest sense of the word, and we were, in turn, absorbing it on a cellular level. He was also incredibly intuitive in the most remarkable way. One time, I saw Dr. Lad look at a woman's fingernail and say, "Oh, my dear. I'm so sorry. When you were younger, your grandmother got into a car accident, and it still scars you today." In the Jewish tradition, it is believed that there are at least twenty-six sages of wisdom walking on this planet at any given time. If that's true, there's a good argument that Dr. Lad is one of them. He embodies a tremendous amount of healing power.

It was clear to me that everyone at the institute—students and teachers alike—shared a very clear objective to better their own lives and the lives of those around them. This objective resonated deeply with me. It felt like a path had opened up, and I knew I had to dive in and learn more. Perhaps most of all, being at the institute made me realize that I could start my life totally fresh. That realization felt profound because there weren't a lot of paths open to me at that point, and none of the traditional ones appealed to me. It felt as if I had just come out of a war zone and could no longer relate to normal society. The Ayurvedic Institute and, more generally, the study of Ayurveda, felt like something I could do to heal and provide direction in my life moving forward. My mom left a little bit of money to my siblings and me, so I used my portion to enroll at the Ayurvedic Institute and buy a used Chevy Tahoe.

At the time, moving to Albuquerque to study Ayurveda was an unusual thing to do. Today, most people have probably heard of Ayurveda or are, at the very least, aware of alternative and Eastern medicines. Back then, the people I told were like, "What's that—Chinese medicine or something?" That didn't deter me though.

I arrived in Albuquerque about a year after my mom's death. New Mexico is an interesting place. A friend once explained the experience of living in New Mexico as similar to an existence in which you're surrounded by mirrors. That beautiful, arid, expansive land somehow breeds self-reflection, and you see things about yourself there that you couldn't before. It's also a place of contrast. On the one hand, New Mexico is home to a number of dilapidated tribal Native American compounds where alcoholism runs rampant. On the other hand, it is a land of spiritual calling where seekers and artists flock to find refuge.

I arrived at the institute before school started and asked if there was any work I could do to make some cash. I was told they needed some landscaping to get the school ready. Unfortunately, they didn't have a lot of tools, so I literally spent those first few weeks using my hands to dig up rocks from deep under the soil as the New Mexico sun beat down on me. I remember looking down at my hands and thinking how symbolic it was, this physical act of digging in deep and pulling the heaviness out. I also remember thinking how necessary this strenuous effort was to create space for healthy, nutrient-rich crops.

Once classes started, I learned that most of my classmates were former executives in their fifties or sixties who had already climbed the corporate ladder and realized it wasn't for them. In the wake of this, they were looking for a new identity and more meaning. They had plenty of money to burn in the process of doing so. As a twenty-one-year-old who was making a big investment that I couldn't really afford, I was different. I was the youngest person in my class by at least fifteen years. So many times, my classmates told me how lucky I was to be so young and already seeking.

They're right: I was lucky on that count.

I was also broke, so I lived very humbly. I slept on an egg crate and worked my ass off, studying full time while also working four different jobs cleaning houses, working in hospitality, and at the Ayurvedic Institute itself. In the little downtime I had, I played music on my turntables to get into the zone. Sometimes I drove up north to Santa Fe, where I hiked up to beautiful hot springs. There wasn't a trail or anything like that. You had to venture on your own, which I especially liked to do on nights when there was a full moon.

Every student at the institute was asked to sign a contract agreeing to put the Ayurvedic way of life into practice. This included a list of commitments such as not drinking, eating a vegetarian diet, and going to bed at a particular time every night. Several months into my first year, one of the administrators asked if I wanted to go out to get pizza and beer and shoot pool with a group of fellow students.

"I'm just curious," I responded. "Is that okay? Because the contract said we're not supposed to drink."

"Oh, you read the contract?" She laughed.

I ended up skipping that night out. Yes, I am a huge nerd, but it goes to show how dedicated to and serious about the program I was. There was a niche group among the thirty of us that were really into the deeper aspects of yoga, plant medicine, and Ayurveda. Obviously, I was one of those people. Many other students saw their time at the institute as more of an adjunct mode of healing or break from life.

There's a saying in *Pirkei Avot*, an ancient Jewish text, that goes, "Find yourself a teacher, acquire yourself a friend." This was basically my motto in life. Based on my background, it felt important to find a wise teacher, as well as friends that I could learn and grow with. Dr. Lad was everything I'd hoped he would be and soon became not just a teacher and mentor to me but also like a father. He was someone who I could look up to and strive to emulate in my search to find more depth and meaning in life.

To this day, I feel so lucky that Dr. Lad was the first teacher I found in the healing arts space. As I got older and continued my studies in health and wellness and holistic arts, I saw firsthand how easy it can be to be misled down a dangerous path by a misguided teacher who claims to be a master or guru. It's easy for people who are desperate and searching for real meaning and value to be scammed. I've seen it happen plenty of times. While Dr. Lad was a lot of things to me, he was not a guru. Likewise, although my training in Ayurveda was part of my personal spiritual journey, I didn't misunderstand it as being a religious practice. In fact, Ayurveda emerged before many religious traditions did and is all about health and wellness without an attached religious agenda. Yes, the goal of Ayurveda is to find a deeper sense of connectivity, but it isn't deity-based. Dr. Lad stayed very true to the heart of Ayurveda's teachings in this regard. As he put it, "If you see a sign pointing to Santa Fe, you don't stop to offer flowers to and worship the sign. You go in the direction the sign is pointing." This was Dr. Lad's way of explaining that he was not special or sacred unto himself; he was merely passing along information that was.

In addition to bringing me into Dr. Lad's orbit, the institute also afforded me the opportunity to make a lot of friends who helped me walk a better path in life than I probably would have otherwise. Since pretty much all of my classmates were significantly older than me, I asked them a lot of questions that most people would discuss with their parents about things like career plans and relationships. I got a lot of great advice from them that I took forward with me into life.

One of the things I loved most about the institute is that it wasn't run like any other classroom I'd ever been in. First of all, it was small. All of our education took place in a single room that was strewn with pillows with a sort of chairback. We students spread out on our pillows, gathered around Dr. Lad as he sat down on the floor cross-legged to teach. He talked to us rather than *at* us, imparting the information he had learned over his lifetime and explaining why it mattered and how to apply it in practice. It wasn't about taking notes and memorizing for the sake of the teacher's agenda. It wasn't about how much information we could cram into our brains and then regurgitate in order to earn a grade. Instead, we learned based on the oral tradition through which Ayurveda has spread over the past five thousand years. Also, our learning didn't stop in the classroom. We had context because we lived and breathed the Ayurvedic methodology from morning until night—it was an all-intensive, experiential, 360-degree form of learning, which allowed the information to seep into our bones.

Ayurveda revolves around the five major elements—fire, water, earth, air, and space—as they interact with and exist within a person. The practice is based on the notion that the world on the inside (the human body) works similarly to the world on the outside (the elements). Combined, these elements provide a complete picture of a person's internal state. Fire refers to a person's brightness, light, clarity, and digestive and metabolic properties. An individual's level of internal fire dictates the vibrancy of their thoughts, words, and actions. Then there's water. Human beings are a reflection of the earth we live on, including the fact that the internal salt/water ratio in humans is the same as that of the ocean. Also, like our planet, each of us is made up of 80 percent water, which smooths and softens the body, and also allows us to move through life with fluidity and grace. The earth element refers to a person's substance mass, bone density, and strength. Air is the flow and movement an individual experiences.

Lack of sufficient air is associated with dry or brittle qualities, which often manifest themselves in the nails and hair. Space is necessary for the different parts of the body to communicate. For example, for neurons to send signals at light speed, there needs to exist a small space between one neuron and the next so that communication can happen efficiently. It's a lot like how we require space in our daily interactions. If we lack the proper amount of space between ourselves and others, it can cause difficulty in communication and disruption that leads to irritability and anxiety.

These five elements bond together within us human beings, coming together as a metabolic type. Physically, they manifest as hair and eye color, skin tone, body shape, muscle mass, and bone density. Based on these elements, Ayurveda breaks people into three types, which are referred to as *doshas*. *Vata* types feature air and space as their prominent elements. *Pitta* personalities feature fire and water. *Kapha* features water and earth. Of course, we all have each of these elements within us, but a person's dosha is determined according to how they balance those five different elements within their constitution. Certain physical and personality characteristics tend to go with each dosha.

Physically, vatas are often wide-eyed and fall on the thin, wispy side. They tend to have a wiry frame and long extremities, dry skin and hair, and brittle nails. Vatas can have an erratic appetite, be restless, and experience trouble sleeping. Vatas are often more spiritually inclined and generally fun and excited about life. They can also be flighty and forget things quickly. With that, vatas tend to be very forgiving. Vatas are drawn to dry, brittle, and cold foods.

Physically, pittas tend to be angular; have a more athletic build; bright, vibrant eyes; and shiny hair. Those with a pitta dosha are passionate. They tend to be competitive and are driven by a sense of accomplishment. Pittas like to be right, and they often verbalize that desire. We definitely see a lot of this dosha type in the Western culture. Pittas can easily build up too much heat through their fire and drive, and this needs to be balanced; otherwise, it can present as too much stomach acid or heat in the blood. They are often attracted to salty, sour, and spicy foods.

Physically, kaphas tend to have a fuller body with thicker bones. They have thicker hair, thick and oily skin, and a thick, lustrous voice. They are not drawn to exercise and are slower to speak. Kapha personalities might take a few times to digest information, but once they've got it, they will never forget it. Kaphas can be phenomenal friends and coworkers because they are loyal and dedicated, both to their relationships and to their craft. Hurt a kapha once, and it's okay; hurt them twice, and they'll get over it; but hurt a kapha three times, and they're done. Kaphas often gravitate to soft, sweet foods and have a slow but steady appetite.

A person's dosha might change as they move through different phases of their life and/or be present at various degrees of extremity. Also, different stages of life are associated with different doshas. With their cuteness, sweet eyes, and vibrant shininess, babies are very kapha-like in nature. Once hormones and high heat kick in during the teens, we tend to hold a lot of pitta energy. And vata is often associated with the later stages of life when people's bone density decreases, and they begin to figure out ways to slow down and give back.

At first, it might sound a bit strange to drill down to such specific tastes and food preferences, but one of the underlying philosophies of Ayurveda is that we must be aware and cognizant about what we put into our bodies and how nutrition transforms itself into energy. Food and botanicals can help address and alleviate imbalances in our dosha because, just like humans, food and botanicals also contain the five elements within them. When we consume food or a sip on a tea or botanical, our bodies transform that energy into its full potential, thanks to the human body's incredible ability to alchemize (more on that in just a minute).

Ayurveda focuses not only on what we should eat based on our constitution but also on the way we combine foods. I believe I was predisposed to this particular element of the philosophy since the idea of kosher eating is built into my Jewish background. Although ayurvedic eating practices and kosher eating are not the same, the general concept made sense to me. Throughout my life, I've found that whenever a basic idea exists in different philosophies or cultures, there's usually some sort of universal wisdom and truth to it. I'm personally more focused on universal wisdom than any specific belief.

I learned so many incredible things through my studies at the institute, like how each and every one of us is an internal alchemist. Herbs in a bowl don't do anything, but ingest them into the body, and their effect is profound. Even more impressive is the body's ability to compound the effects of various herbs. For example, if you were to take two herbs like echinacea and goldenseal on their own, they each would work fine for their intended purpose (to help increase the efficiency of the immune system and support the thyroid and body's natural healing ability, respectively). Combine them together, though, and they will have a compounded effect on your antibacterial and microbial properties. In other words, together, these two herbs build upon one another and become an incredibly powerful tool for health and wellness.

This compounding effect happens thanks to the human body's ability to transform herbs in tandem. You literally have an internal engine for alchemy. You can think of it like this: look at your computer keyboard, and you'll see a collection of letters, numbers, and symbols. Hit any individual key, and all it does is display that specific letter, number, or symbol on your screen. But combine those keystrokes in the correct sequence, and you can enter in a password that opens up powerful tools, which are then at your disposal to use in any number of ways. Similarly, the right formulation and amounts of herbs and botanicals can unlock a deep potential within the person who ingests them.

I also learned about the importance of space and energy when it comes to working with herbs. I learned how much environment matters—including everything from the time and space in which herbs are blended all the way down to the direction in which they are stirred. Stirring in a clockwise direction brings the energy of herbs up; it's additive. To draw something out of a blend—for instance, an unappealing fragrance—the herb is stirred counterclockwise.

Never before had I learned so much information that was directly applicable to my life experience in just a few months' time. At the end of my first year at the Ayurvedic Institute, there was a question on the final exam that I still remember to this day. It was: "What is the definition of karma?" We had studied karma throughout the year, and there was a textbook answer to this question. But the answer I gave in that moment wasn't taken from the pages of our textbook. Instead, I offered this: "Karma is the way in which how you think today affects how you think and act tomorrow." At the time, I didn't know that this answer would live on inside of me and become a major driver in my life, particularly from a business point of view.

In between my first and second years at the institute, I decided to do yoga teacher training at a beautiful institute tucked away high up in the majestic redwood forests of the Santa Cruz Mountains. I thought that, maybe at some point in the future, I would open up a treatment center that fused together yoga and Ayurveda. I come from a family of therapists and speak their language, so I considered this potential treatment center to be a practice of sorts. So, before enrolling in the yoga program, I called up the director and asked if this training would help me open up a practice.

"Absolutely!" he answered. "I'm so thrilled you asked that. I wish more people would."

I completed the training that summer, and it was amazing. But I was confused. By the end of the training, we hadn't even remotely touched on the process of opening up a practice. I went up to the teacher and said, "We didn't discuss advertising, marketing, or setting up a practice at all. I was told we were going to learn about opening up a practice here."

I'm sure it was all the teacher could do to keep from laughing in my face because, of course, yogis use the word *practice* as it pertains to their movement both on and off the mat—*not* to the logistics of a therapeutic business.

Still, the experience was profoundly valuable. I slept in a tent on the campus, which was alive with wild deer scampering all over the place. It was immersed in what felt like a bubble of lush, majestic redwoods and misty mountains. There was a special energy to the environment that soaked into me. I felt a deep sense of being alive.

I worked on campus to help pay my way through teacher training, just as I had at the Ayurvedic Institute. There was a farm on campus, and all of the produce we ate was grown on-site. I worked in the kitchen, as well as doing some gardening work. This was great for me because we practiced Ayurvedic cooking, which allowed me to deepen my experience in Ayurveda by learning to apply it to practical living on a larger scale. There was also an Ayurvedic component to the yoga teacher program training itself, and I was proud and honored when I was asked to help teach that section of the training.

As part of his belief in conserving his energy for faith, the leader of the teacher training program had taken a vow of silence. By the time I arrived at the school, he hadn't spoken in fifty-five years. In the classroom, he wrote lessons on either a big chalkboard in the room or on a mini chalkboard that he wore around his neck. To supplement this, his teaching assistants helped teach the class by explaining his lessons in detail. Because of this, in addition to the yoga teacher training, some people came to the center to do silent retreats for a week at a time. While I was there, I decided to give it a try for a day. A day might not sound like a long time to remain in silence, but man, I learned a lot in that short period of time, and many of those lessons have stuck with me ever since. I learned what it really means to be silent. In that twenty-four-hour period, I noticed that people kept coming up to talk to me because they knew I couldn't talk back. It showed me how much people just want to be listened to. Ever since then, I have tried to be a careful, intentional listener.

It was also a profound experience to speak again after those twenty-four hours were up. I was so much more aware of the act of speaking, specifically, of the vibration speaking caused in my throat and chest. I could feel everything reverberating throughout my body as I talked. It was an incredibly powerful experience that reminded me in a very sensory way of the power of my words and the energy that I was devoting to the act of bringing those words into the world.

I returned to my second year at the Ayurvedic Institute feeling even more confident in what I was doing and who I was becoming. I was also excited because, since the second year was designed for advanced students, we got to dive deeper into Sanskrit texts and see patients with Dr. Lad. Even as the year began, my mind turned toward what I was going to do once my time at the institute was over. I knew that New Mexico was not the place for me in the long term.

My hard work wasn't lost on the teachers at the institute, and beyond that, I think they could also see how deeply curious I was about the constitutional effects of various botanicals. I wanted to understand every element of how herbology worked and was serious and strict in my practice, including everything from sourcing to blending to packing.

Along with its educational program, the institute also housed a treatment center and pharmacy on campus. The treatment center was renowned, and people from all over came to visit. Many people turned to the institute's treatment center when they reached a point where more traditional modalities had failed them. For some, it was a last resort. It was incredible to see how this population of patients transformed, often in as little as two-weeks' time. We also had our fair share of celebrities, despite the fact that the treatment center was far from a flashy five-star resort. It was intense, a place where people came to do real work and deep healing.

And then there was the herbal pharmacy—one of the most important and formative places I have ever set foot in. During my second year at the institute, I was chosen as the only student advanced enough to work on blending and sourcing alongside the masters at my school. To put my experience there into context, it's important to understand that, of the thirty people who were in my first-year class, only about ten of us made it into the advanced program the following year. Some had to repeat the first year again, and others walked away altogether. While it was an untraditional educational experience in the Western sense, it was stringent. We were presented with a lot of knowledge to absorb, but once we internalized the information, it was phenomenally useful. For example, we learned to diagnose people's ailments and deficiencies simply by talking to them and looking at their faces or tongues. The tongue acts as a sensor and is like a mirror into the internal system—it's amazing how much information is encoded there. It makes for a cool experience and an awesome party trick—*if* people are open to it. But at the time (especially back when my skills were really honed), it was also intense. Sometimes it can feel like a burden to see what's *really* going on with people, especially because I wanted to help but never wanted to force my help on them.

Being allowed to work in the on-campus pharmacy was a huge honor because it was considered a sacred space. No one was allowed inside of it, with the exception of myself and a couple of master blenders and herbalists who had worked there for years and been trained under Dr. Lad. While the rules for being in the room were stringent, the room itself was very Zen, very intentional, and very protective. My job was to source and formulate the herbs we worked on.

Back then, sourcing herbs was an entirely different beast than it is today. The internet was still nascent, and Amazon was new, and only for books at that. This meant that I spent a lot of my time searching through old phone books and calling vendors in various parts of Asia to locate botanicals. It was one of those phone calls that ultimately led me to want to start sourcing herbs myself.

After a diligent search, I had sourced some gingko and was on the phone with the supplier. I was trying to be as efficient as possible because, back then, long-distance was a thing, and I knew this call was costing the institute two dollars per minute.

The supplier on the other end of the line asked me if I wanted gingko from the western or eastern slope of the river.

"It doesn't matter," I told him. "I just need to order gingko."

"No, sir," he said kindly. "It does matter. Perhaps you need to come here yourself to understand why."

I was intrigued. I had no clue why it mattered what slope of the river the gingko was grown on, which told me that I was missing an important piece of information. Today, I understand that it matters because the position of the sun and water impact both the flavor and medicinal properties of the botanical. I also understand that these details are *so* important that, in some cases, an herb or botanical that grows on one side of the water may not grow at all on the other.

But I didn't yet know that then. All I knew was that I needed to start saving up my money so that I could travel to where the botanicals were grown and learn more firsthand.

I continued my education in Ayurveda that second year, but the majority of my attention was focused on the pharmacy. That's where I learned the most. I also continued working additional jobs on the side, cleaning houses and working as a waiter late at night, so that I could save up for whatever came next.

My time at the Ayurvedic Institute represented a pivotal turning point in my life. Graduation felt like a significant rite of passage, and it also felt liberating. Not only had I learned so much and begun to carve out the beginnings of a path for myself, but just as importantly, those two years had allowed me to begin to heal, observe, reflect, and find my own direction.

I was excited to go out and start sharing and applying the knowledge I had acquired in my time at the institute with the world, but I also still had a lot to figure out. The fact of the matter is that in the 1990s, the world wasn't very interested in a twenty-something who didn't have a traditional four-year degree. Much less in one with an education from an alternative health program in New Mexico.

I had found my direction, but the road was still uncertain.

CHAPTER THREE

SEARCHING

I left New Mexico knowing that my next goal was to backpack the world. I wanted to see for myself what conditions made for the best possible herbs and botanicals.

A friend of mine was in a now defunct Peace Corps–type of program called Otzma (which means "strength" in Hebrew). She suggested that I join and go to Israel. "I think you can make a big impact," she said. "What you understand about horticulture and stress management could definitely be put to use there."

I was in.

I joined the program, and off to Israel I went for the next year. In addition to the opportunities to learn and have an impact, Israel appealed to me because I felt called to dive into my roots.

Parts of Israel are stunning, with incredible landscapes and beaches, ancient castles, and captivating bodies of water that are associated with early history that dates back thousands of years. The parts of Israel I went to (Sderot and Kiryat Malachi) weren't like that at all. If anything, they reminded me of Tijuana. Both towns bordered Gaza and were continually bombed. As a result, the areas were extremely underdeveloped and dilapidated, boasting one streetlight in the entire town.

But what they lacked in aesthetics and public resources, they made up for in heart. The people were loving and kind. Everyone was constantly out and about on the streets, making eye contact with one another. While the landscape might not have been rich, the culture certainly was.

I learned to speak Hebrew so that I could communicate more effectively. Otzma offered us a three-month language course, but I struggled to absorb Hebrew in that setting. Instead, I decided to take to the streets and learn Hebrew in a real-world setting.

One of the primary places I practiced was at the market, where I forced myself to interact in ways that felt vulnerable as I waded my way through all of the many flavors and spices up for offer. Thankfully, I found that the locals I interacted with were very warmhearted and forgiving. In the end, I built my understanding of the Hebrew language largely upon spice and vegetable stands.

Otzma placed me in the home of a local family, who I lived with for the duration of the year. They were warm and loving, and the experience of being part of that type of household was profoundly healing for me. My host family did things no one had done for me since I was twelve. They washed my laundry, took me on field trips, and accepted and embraced me as one of their own. They gave me the opportunity to understand what growing up in a healthy family could look and feel like. In the moment, I'm not sure I realized how much I needed that experience, but I certainly understood that it felt very good. Being around them inspired me to want to build a happy, healthy family of my own.

My assignment in Israel was to teach horticulture for one part of the day and yoga for the other part of the day at different programs throughout the community. The first thing I noticed upon arriving for my assignment was how malnourished a lot of the kids were. I noticed that one child, in particular, ate a pita for breakfast, lunch, and dinner every single day. I asked one of the teachers why that was, and she replied that it was because the student didn't have anything else. This opened my eyes and inspired me to build an herb and vegetable garden with students at one of the local schools to help alleviate the chronic malnourishment that so many of them suffered from. I wanted to leave something behind that would allow these children to help themselves for a long time to come. I also participated in a lot of peace program projects designed to bring Arabs and Israelis together. In addition to that, I also wrote and directed a play for the children to perform. Much like when I had been a camp counselor, I wanted to do it all.

I spent that year soaking in whatever opportunities came my way. Looking back on that time in my life, I can clearly see how even the darkest experiences leave gifts in their wake. One of the gifts of losing my mom when she was still so young is that I witnessed firsthand how limited our time here can be. It sparked in me the desire to drink from the fountain of life as much as possible. At a core level, I wanted to make the most of the time I had and to maximize the energy I extended.

In addition to teaching horticulture while in Israel, I also explored what the land and culture had to offer in the way of herbs and botanicals. I poured through a number of ancient texts that illuminated what my long-ago ancestors had believed about health and wellness and what their approach had been via sacred texts. I learned some interesting things about what the ancient Jewish tradition believed about the physical and spiritual connection and how they saw food, herbs, and timing of teas as an integral element.

The work I was doing with the program was all done on a volunteer basis, so as usual, I took on odd jobs to pay the bills, which set me apart from my fellow volunteers. Since we were all recent college graduates, pretty much all of the other volunteers were able to supplement their living with the help of their parents. Of course, this wasn't the case for me, so I worked as a cook to bring in some extra money. I used that work as an opportunity to incorporate some of my Ayurvedic knowledge in practical ways.

Israel was an important experience for me because it allowed me to connect. Being an early twenty-something who has suffered grief and loss can be an isolating experience because so few of your peers can relate. Even close friends can struggle to understand where you're coming from and what you're going through. I found it a challenging position to be in. In Israel, though, people of all ages had a deep understanding of suffering, grief, and loss. Multiple wars and terrorist attacks colored their view of life in a way that I resonated deeply with. Living through circumstances like this prompted many of the people I crossed paths with to intentionally seek out a life of value and purpose.

In Israel, a tribe of people gathered from all over the world—everywhere from Morocco, from Poland, from South Africa—precisely because they had been through a series of hardships that involved not belonging or being evicted from their homeland. This led the people of Israel to value their community and place in life in a way I had never before witnessed. This resonated deeply with me as well.

Being immersed in this sort of culture inspired me to double down on my philosophy that the next day is always going to be a better one. It solidified my belief that even the most painful experiences in life allow us the opportunity to observe, learn, and grow. It made me even more acutely aware of the fact that we are all on this earth for but a limited time, and it's nothing short of critical that we embrace and maximize that time to the best of our ability. In Israel, I felt welcomed and embraced for who I was. I felt good about myself because I knew I could add value to their lives as well.

I walked away from Israel with a deep and true understanding of how healing community can be, of how community can be an almost spiritual experience. I came away with an entirely new perspective about living in the moment. I remember walking through a park with a friend around 10:30 one night and seeing a group of people gather to begin a salsa class. There was a wide range of them, running the gamut from eighty-year-olds to twenty-year-olds.

"What's this all about?" I asked my friend. "It's pretty late for salsa class, isn't it?"

"When you live in a country that's at war," she explained, "you never know what tomorrow is going to bring. We're here today, and we're going to live as much as we possibly can."

I think it's also because of this that, in Israel, strangers can become friends very quickly. Being around that kind of openness broke me out of my insular shell. It allowed me to focus less intently on healing, cleansing, and growth and, instead, to simply allow myself to have fun and connect on a human level.

These lessons and shifts landed all the more deeply in me because my connection with these beautiful people happened as I was simultaneously connecting with a new sense of purpose and my personal history. Coming from America, I was moved by the experience of being in a culture that embraces history over technology. In New Mexico, a building from the 1870s is considered old. In Israel, the stones that Jesus walked on two thousand years ago are still in place. All of it gave me a deeper sense of who I was and where I came from.

After twelve months in Israel, I returned to LA as an entirely different person than I had been when I left three years before. I still didn't know exactly what I was going to do with my life, but Israel had given me more direction. It was clear to me that I felt driven to impact the world through wellness and community. I felt torn about what that looked like though. On the one hand, everything that I had learned at the Ayurvedic Institute continued to compel me and light me on fire. On the other hand, Israel had made me wonder if perhaps a rabbinical path was the best way forward for me.

Back on American soil, I quickly realized that my main struggle with incorporating Ayurveda into a professional scenario was that, plain and simple, I felt weird seeing patients. I met with a few and found that I became so emotionally connected to their well-being that it felt wrong to charge them any money, despite the many hours I spent with them. I deeply felt the desire to assist these people but quickly understood that I needed to find another way to teach them how to help themselves outside of a consultation practice. Dr. Lad's words rang in my ears: "If you see someone slipping in the mud, you hand them a stick, not your hand. If you give them a stick, they will have a tool they can climb out with. Give them your hand, and they will pull you in." I also had to figure out how to protect myself so that I didn't get sucked into whatever troubles a person was going through. As time went by, I continued to do Ayurvedic consultation work intermittently, but I never felt good about charging people money for health and wellness on that sort of individual basis.

Once I realized this, I accepted a job at Vista Del Mar Child and Family Services, which was a high-quality treatment program for children with significant emotional, social, learning, and developmental disabilities. Although I wasn't ordained, I more or less worked as a Rabbi at Vista Del Mar, providing spiritual counseling for the kids. During my time in Israel, I had spent a lot of time learning in *yeshiva*. Yeshiva is an intensive and immersive learning program where one grapples with life scenarios, laws, and religious outlooks. It strengthens and stretches the mind and soul. This study felt similar to what I had experienced at the Ayurvedic Institute, insofar as that I absorbed ancient teachings (and interpretations of those ancient teachings) orally. In Israel, that consisted of learning the teachings side by side with another student and then engaging in a passionate debate about the meaning and lessons of those texts.

I resonated deeply with the dozens of children from broken homes who lived at Vista Del Mar. Because I had been through hard times in my own young life, I was able to help lift them out of a victim mentality and raise them up to a place where they could see opportunity in their own lives. I worked with them to find ways in which they could alchemize their pain into growth, a meaningful life, and perhaps even a source of inspiration.

During my time at Vista Del Mar, I assumed that I would eventually go to rabbinical school. This path made sense for me for so many reasons, including the fact that, in addition to spiritual matters, Judaism also focuses a lot on health and wellness.

I also continued traveling during this time. One of my most significant adventures was to an area called the Golden Triangle, which includes Northern Thailand, Laos, and Cambodia. I made the trip because I wanted to learn more about the botanicals in the area.

In Laos, I rented a moped and was riding through rice paddies when I happened upon a little French bakery that sold tea leaves wrapped in string. I'd never seen anything like these sticks. They were simultaneously cool and gross—the leaves were so fresh and of the earth that they still had dirt on them. If you've ever seen a sage smudge stick, the bundled tea leaves looked a lot like that. Brewing these leaves into tea involved nothing more than breaking a bit of tea off of the stick and steeping it in water.

Unbeknownst to me at the time, this tea was very special because that area of Laos houses some of the most ancient tea trees. These trees are so well entrenched in the land that they often produce beautiful leaves even in the absence of rainfall because their roots run so deep. Generally speaking, the trees in tea fields are well trimmed, but these ancient trees that were left largely unattended could grow up to ten feet tall! Traditionally, women climb large ladders to collect the leaves because they tend to have a more delicate touch than men and are able to collect the tea without bruising the leaves.

I'd never tasted anything like this tea before, although admittedly, my experience with tea was very limited at that time. I'd only ever drunk poor-quality supermarket-grade tea, which did nothing for me. This cup of tea woke me up, though—it was *amazing*, and I figured there had to be a whole world out there that I was unaware of. I was intrigued.

I asked the woman who ran the bakery about these leaves and where they had come from. She told me she'd gotten the leaves from a local farmer. Despite my probing questions, she was vague about who the farmer was, so I set off on my moped with no information other than the general direction she pointed me in. I didn't even really know what I was looking for because I had no idea what tea fields even looked like at the time.

My interest was sparked. When I came back home, I started searching the internet for tea like I'd found at that bakery. I came up empty. There was just one online store at the time, and all it had were these funky, bizarre tea cakes—not what I was looking for.

I knew there had to be more out there, even if I didn't know how to find it. I started to wonder if there was an opportunity in tea, along the lines of an epicurean, high-quality food experience.

Something else pivotal happened during these years: I met the woman who I would eventually marry, Leetal. Like me, she loved to travel, so we embarked on a series of adventures together. To this day, we're still adventuring.

In 2004, Leetal and I got married and spent our honeymoon driving across both islands of New Zealand. In every way, that time was a transition point. It was the bridge between single life and married life, and also a professional fork in the road. Going into our honeymoon, I knew that I had two options before me, both of which were viable: to become a Rabbi or to open a tea business. Shortly before our marriage, I had been offered a rabbinical position that came with a six-figure salary. I was definitely drawn to the opportunity—it felt impactful and purpose-driven.

The idea of opening a tea company, on the other hand, felt bold and daring. I loved that tea would allow me to utilize all of the Ayurvedic knowledge I had acquired to help people enhance their health and wellness in a way that didn't involve one-on-one counseling. Tea allowed a delicious delivery method for all of the botanicals I believed so deeply in. I felt that I could impact people through tea, albeit in a different way than I would impact people as a Rabbi. It occurred to me that I might be able to impact *more* people through tea than I could as a Rabbi. But of course, there was no guarantee of success—financial or otherwise.

Leetal and I had ample driving time as we explored New Zealand's lush forests, desert landscapes, and frigid ocean waters, so we downloaded and listened to a ton of Tony Robbins. When I think back to that trip, I think of his voice. The things Tony had to say about leading an authentic, purpose-driven life with as much intention as possible really struck a chord with me. Also, as someone who believes deeply in the value of mentors, I loved that his information and advice were the distilled best practices of some of the world's most notable CEOs, athletes, leaders, and great minds.

One day as we were driving, Leetal turned to me and said, "You know, you're really good at what you do. You can always go back to rabbinical work if you decide you want to, but you might never have another opportunity to start this tea company you've been dreaming of."

She was right. The two of us knew that we wanted kids—and in fact, we found out that we were pregnant with our first child just six months later. But in that moment, we were still untethered from some of the responsibility that we knew was just around the bend. As we discussed what this might look like, we calculated that if I could make even $1,000 per week (50 or 60 percent of which would go toward products), we'd be okay. I could run the company myself and, perhaps at some point down the line, bring someone else on to help me as necessary.

I made the decision on that trip to go for it, to decline the opportunity to lead a congregation and community and, instead, start a tea company. It seemed like this was the moment. I knew that if I didn't try now, I probably never would—and I felt pretty sure that I would regret that in the long run.

I was excited about so many different elements of opening a tea company. I loved teaching in general, and I particularly loved teaching people about the historical context of tea and how it has transformed our world (turn to Chapter 6 for more on that). There aren't many anchors to our collective past amongst all cultures in the world today, but tea is one of them. The ritual of drinking tea on the porch with your grandma in Chicago today is very similar to drinking tea as a ritual in Japan a few hundred years ago. On a more personal level, tea wove together so many of the things I cared about the most: health, wellness, and spirituality. I also loved the fact that tea didn't spiritually discriminate. It had nothing to do with traditional religion, and its impact cut across all of the divides that existed in so many other areas of life, including age, socioeconomics, and gender.

Aside from my own passion for herbology and tea and seeing an opening in the market from a business point of view, I also saw a way that I could make a real impact in people's lives through tea. We live in a world that is constantly on a quest for new technology. There are definitely some benefits to this. But I believe there is also something incredibly special about timeless wisdom and products, craftsmanship, and some analog time to slow us down in the fast-paced world where we live. Tea does all of this.

That doesn't mean that I didn't have some reservations. I had plenty of them. I spent a lot of time questioning whether or not opening a tea company was the right move. Did it really make sense to enter into a space people hadn't already flocked to? I wasn't sure that it did. What if *I* didn't have what it took to found a viable business? What if I opened a company that didn't make it?

But every time, I kept coming back to the one I *did* know for sure, which is that every single time I sat down to drink tea, I felt something shift inside of me. I felt more vibrant, both metabolically and physiologically. I felt a greater sense of clarity. If I was reaping the benefits of the timeless wisdom that goes into good tea and if people had spent thousands of years embracing it into their culture, didn't there have to be something to it? Wasn't this a way that I could impact the Western world in even a small way?

In the end, I thought that tea just might be that road toward impact.

CHAPTER FOUR

THE ART OF TEA

As I began taking those first steps toward opening my own business, I continued working part time at Vista Del Mar, which provided me with a sense of security to temper the risk. For the first year, my little venture existed in our living room. As I blended the teas and botanicals I had collected throughout my travels in the previous years, I relied on the knowledge I had acquired both at the institute and on my own in the ensuing years. I dedicated myself to blending the most beautiful and delicious teas possible, while also paying attention to how the ingredients would compound in the body for maximum benefit. My goal was to pack in ingredients that not only tasted compelling but that also carried potency and the potential to transform the drinker on a deeper level. To this day, that's still the goal.

Much as Dr. Lad had viewed his own work, I looked at this endeavor of mine as both a craft and an art. During this period, I read Sun Tzu's *The Art of War*, from which I extracted a lot of timeless strategies that I applied to my own work. A few of the philosophies in that book really stood out to me. I was drawn to the idea that opportunities multiply as they are won. I was also fascinated by the idea that there are not more than five musical notes, primary colors, or tastes, and yet the combinations of these basics give rise to infinite melodies, hues, and flavors. That reminded me of tea and the way in which this one type of leaf that *all* teas are derived from (*Camellia sinensis*) could be transformed into so many different tastes, depending upon how the leaves are grown, processed, cooked, massaged, rolled, and blended. I read about how *gong fu,* the practice of preparing and pouring tea multiple times until it's just right, was derived from the martial art of kung fu, and I began to think of tea as a martial art. This served as the inspiration for my company's name: Art of Tea.

I see tea as a connector, which makes it a great fit for the hospitality industry. Rather than selling my teas on the open market, my plan was to distribute my creations to restaurants and hotels. As I started to brainstorm this B2B model, I wanted to research how other tea companies were distributing. At one point, I ventured out of my living room to visit a shop in Santa Monica that sold beautiful, high-quality teas, among other things. I spoke to a gentleman who worked there and told him about my new business, including the fact that I was thinking about selling to restaurants. "It's not worth it for you," he replied. "I sell to all of the restaurants in LA."

Disheartened, I left the store and flipped my phone open to call Leetal. "I don't know if I should do this," I told her. I explained that the man I had just spoken to sold tea to all of the restaurants in LA.

"*All* of the restaurants in LA?" she asked dubiously. "You have something great to offer. Keep going."

Two weeks later, I drove by that same store in Santa Monica and saw that it was shut down forever. This was a great lesson for me that even when I'm worried I might fail at something, it's important to try a few times before backing down.

So many of the early days were like that—a mixture of doubt and inspiration. I quickly learned to take it one day at a time, and those days included a constant dialogue between my wife and me as I voiced my worries about whether or not this could really work. All the while, I kept blending and packing in our living room.

When I felt confident enough in my creations, I purchased a camera bag that had a lot of different compartments intended for lenses and film containers. I used those compartments to store a glass teapot and tea samples and lugged that bag around town. Much as I had done when I was fourteen years old, I knocked on people's doors and asked for business. I understood that I would get plenty of nos, so I steeled myself against rejection and constantly reminded myself that every no was getting me closer to a yes. My job was to show up and do the work; beyond that, the response was out of my control. Even though every visit didn't turn into a sale, people were impressed by the fact that, as a business owner, I was going door to door myself rather than sending a sales representative in my stead. Little did they know, there were no other options! Still, my dedication to Art of Tea resonated with owners and leadership teams of other businesses.

As you can imagine, it was a big deal when I landed my first account with a restaurant. Once I earned that account, I understood that there *was* opportunity for me out there. I just had to keep going and to continue doing the best work I possibly could. So I did. One of the big things I had on my side as I booked those first few accounts is that I didn't come across as a pushy salesman because I believed in my product so truly and deeply. I wasn't selling something I was obligated to sell; I was selling because I felt obligated to give something to the world that I knew would make things better.

During the days, I blended and built up a customer base. At night, I took a web design class at a local community college so that I could create a logo and website for Art of Tea. With my nascent skills, I created the original Art of Tea logo around four o' clock in the morning; it stuck until Art of Tea rebranded in 2016. My cell phone served as customer service, sales, accounts payable and receivable, and also as a hotline that waiters called late at night to let me know when they had a customer who liked the tea and wanted to order some for themselves. I *was* the company. The company budget consisted of a credit card with a $1,000 limit on it. At first, I couldn't believe how much credit was at my disposal, but very quickly, I applied to have the limit raised to $1,500 and then $3,000. Then I applied for another credit card with a $2,500 limit. Those were my first two investors: Uncle Visa and Aunt Mastercard, the balances of which I was constantly juggling (although I made sure to pay them off in full each month!).

One day, I was multitasking, blending teas as I spoke on the phone with a customer from a high-end restaurant who wanted to place an order. In the middle of the conversation, I realized I had accidentally dumped the ingredients meant for one batch of tea into another batch. I had screwed up five pounds of tea, which represented a lot of money for me at the time.

"Shit!" I said, midconversation.

"Excuse me?"

"Oh, no, no, no. Not you!" I cringed.

As soon as I got off the phone, I put the wasted tea into a bag and shoved it into a corner on top of a stack of boxes. A little while later, Leetal walked into the room and noticed the bag.

"What's that?" she asked.

"Oh, it's nothing. I messed up a batch" I told her.

"How do you know you messed it up?" she asked.

"I mean, I'm a tea expert," I told her. "I think I know when I messed up."

"Mmm" she nodded patiently. "Well, you might want to try it, anyway. Just in case"

"It's not going to be good. I don't need to try it, I already know."

But, for some reason, I couldn't get that conversation out of my head. Once I was done being stubborn, I tried the tea as my wife had suggested. What do you know? It was good. In fact, it was really good and went on to become one of Art of Tea's most popular flavors, French Lemon Ginger. Go figure. In the years since then, I've stopped multitasking like I did back then, but I've also seen several other "accidents" become fun, fruitful, new blends.

As the weeks went by, I became more and more obsessed with blending. I kept a journal next to my bed so I could document the recipes that popped into my head in the middle of the night and try them out the next morning. I found inspiration everywhere. One time, in the midst of a monsoon on a trip to Palm Springs, I got out of the car and caught a waft of fresh summer rain. I knew I had to create a tea that smelled just like that. Thus, the Summer Peach blend was born.

Another great example of this is Art of Tea's Mandarin Silk oolong tea. For many years, Leetal was an aesthetician. Because of this, she got samples of all sorts of different creams, soaps, and shampoos. Our shower used to be packed with them. At one point, she had a salt scrub called Mandarin Cashmere. It smelled like a creamy vanilla-citrus blend—sort of like a Creamsicle. I wanted to eat it, and I knew I had to create a tea that mimicked that smell. That scrub ultimately inspired Mandarin Silk, which went on to win a competition for the best oolong in the world. Over the years, Art of Tea has also gone on to create a new category of teas, which we call dessert teas. This includes flavors like Dark Chocolate Peppermint Tea, Butterscotch Tea, and White Coconut Crème, among others. Basically, these flavors are a way for people to have their cake and eat it too—no guilt required!

Even as my little business gathered momentum, I continued to keep the news about the venture to myself. It wasn't until about six months in that I felt ready to start telling my loved ones. My wife and I invited our friends over for a tea party in our backyard. As they sipped their tea, I explained that not only had I made the tea they were drinking but that I was launching a tea company. Up until that point, I had felt too protective of the business to subject it to naysayers, no matter how well-meaning they might be. As I had suspected, the reaction that night was mixed. Some of our friends were really happy, and others were upset. They didn't understand why we had kept Art of Tea a secret for all these months. It was hard to explain to them how I felt—like this business was a precious new tree that I wanted to plant, nurture, and grow before removing the protective fence around it.

As the company continued to grow one little step at a time in those first several months, I decided to travel for a tea conference in Beijing, China. It was important to me to source tea leaves from their origin, in those places where growers and producers have developed a time-tested art and craft. The teas from these points of origin—China, Japan, Taiwan, and India—also have very specific flavor profiles based on the way producers touch and heat the leaves. In my opinion, no one else can get it right in the way these primary countries can. They just have so much practice.

At this conference in Beijing, my goal was to make some connections and, hopefully, to find some suppliers. Prior to this point, I had been relying on some long-time contacts I'd made in the world of botanicals, as well as a couple of suppliers who were already bringing teas into the United States. The quality wasn't quite what I was looking for, though, and I wanted Art of Tea to be a vertically integrated company from source to cup. I was convinced that was the only way I could really tell the story of what each tea was and where it came from, and to be truly transparent about the origin and processing methods of the tea. To me, the story behind a tea is important. I also wanted as few hands as possible on the tea as it made the journey from source to cup. I believed some sort of sacredness was somehow lost when the tea traveled through brokers and distributors.

I embarked on this trip completely convinced that everyone would want to work with me since I was American. I figured they'd be excited to get in on the ground floor in a relatively untapped market. Let's just say that this turned out to be a great opportunity for me to learn about my own ignorance.

My first lesson in ignorance on that trip is that English was not as prevalent as I had believed it would be in Beijing. This proved to be a problem when I attempted to get a ticket into the conference only to realize that no one could understand what I was asking for. Once I finally managed to get my way into the conference, I relearned this lesson time and time again as I walked from one booth to the next.

There was a lot of *pu-erh* being sold at the booths inside of the conference. Pu-erh is an aged, fermented tea. Generally speaking, younger and fresher tea leaves are considered more valuable, but pu-erh is the exception to the rule. It comes from a region in China called the Yunnan province, which is home to six famous mountains. Different families have rights to different parts of the mountains, where they own secret lots on which they harvest the pu-erh. It's a very competitive undertaking.

The problem with pu-erh is that there are a lot of fakes on the market. But when you find the real stuff, it's valuable. I once had a high-profile client come to me in search of pu-erh. I was able to connect with a professor who authorized a batch on behalf of my client. The tea cake, which was no larger than the size of a small frisbee, sold for $2,500. That's pu-erh.

There was a lot of real pu-erh at this particular market, but I needed the guidance of others to learn to determine authenticity and whether or not a pu-erh cake had been baked to mimic aged leaves or had lower-quality leaves mixed in.

As I wandered throughout the stands of pu-erh, I finally ran into a gentleman who spoke some English. When I asked if he was interested in selling to the US, he laughed. "No," he replied. "To be honest, none of us would be interested in selling to you. Why would we be? We have a much larger market here than we would ever have in your country."

That was an eye-opener, but of course, once I heard it, it made sense. Even in India—one of the largest tea producers in the world—more than 70 percent of the product harvested there is sold domestically. The tea market is very dense in the Eastern world.

In that moment, I realized I was climbing an uphill battle. I had to figure out how to create an ecosystem where I could bring teas in from China to the US, despite the various Chinese government compliance regulations. Back then, there were only a couple of government-authorized tea distributors in China (today, it's an open, direct market). This meant that if I was going to buy tea directly from a farm in Asia, I'd have to develop a personal relationship with some of the growers, buy tea onsite, and pack it in a suitcase to bring back to America with me. When I started in this industry, it was possible to import tea direct from growers. Due to enhanced health and safety rules and regulations, this would be much more difficult—if not impossible—today. Especially with the quantities I was bringing in.

After a while, I ran into another man who spoke English. His name was Mr. Huan. When I told Mr. Huan about my plight, he suggested that I go to a tea market. He even offered to take me. I now understand that he was offering protection and connection, introducing me to people who he thought would take care of and do right by me.

After the conference was over, the two of us hopped into a taxi, and I found myself in a place called Tea City. Imagine the largest mall you've ever seen filled with ministalls, each offering tastings and selling different types of tea. The entire market was immersed in the musky smell of cedar and old wood. Everywhere I looked, there were giant bins and piles of white, black, and oolong tea leaves. Women sat on very low stools combing through oolong tea lives in bamboo wicker baskets. They then sorted those leaves based on their size and color variation to sell at different price points based on their grade.

I tried the tea at several stalls in this huge marketplace. Each tasting was prepared in gong fu style—this was the first time I saw the technique up close and personal. Again, there was a lot of pu-erh up for offer. It was an amber color and tasted and smelled a lot like a cognac or scotch, mixed with damp forest floor, camphor, and stinky cheese. There were often three or four other people present, sitting and staring at me as I sipped. In China, it's not considered impolite to stare like it is here. And as a tall, white man, I definitely stood out.

After several of these tastings, Mr. Huan turned to me and said, "Okay, let's go to the next place."

Unbelievably, we walked outside, and I saw that there was another market directly across the street, equally as large as the one we were in. I looked around and realized that there were mall-sized markets chock-full of tea, extending mile after mile as far as the eye could see. In the little alleys in between the malls were tea shops. This staggering number of vendors representing various farms was unlike anything I'd ever seen.

When all was said and done, I spent two days at the market. By the end, I was equal amounts excited and exhausted. It was challenging to navigate that kind of volume and to attempt to digest all of the information that each stand provided me about the history, origin, and distinguishing elements of their tea. And all of this with a massive language barrier! I found myself grateful for the time I'd spent in Israel and how conditioned I'd become to figuring out how to communicate through eye contact, gesturing, kindness, and a smile. It was all very complex, and I knew that I still needed more time to understand the ecosystem, and the best way to do that was to go even more directly to the origin source at the farm level. Many of the stands at these markets were run by farms and families who were growing and producing the teas. But there were also some middlemen, which made navigating the situation somewhat unclear.

From Beijing, I boarded a little plane to travel to the Fujian province, which is home to a lot of green and white teas. In fact, many of the old texts refer to this area as the birthplace of white tea. Sitting next to me on the plane was a fairly young Chinese guy named Alex, who I came to learn was an engineer for a German company headquartered in Beijing. He was headed home to visit his parents in the Fujian province. He spoke English very well, so we got to talking. I explained to Alex what I did and that I was planning on visiting an outdoor tea market to make some connections.

"I'd love to take you around," Alex offered. "I can be your interpreter."

It turns out that Alex's dad was a high government official, so he was able to get me into some places that I wouldn't have had access to as a Westerner. Alex took me up into the hills. I don't get emotional very easily, but going up to those hills and seeing this land that most people from the Western world haven't seen before was a powerful, intoxicating experience that filled me with gratitude and awe. I was taken by the pristine, well-manicured rows of tea leaves in the midst of this cinematic landscape, which was foggy and misty in the earlier part of the day and then sun-drenched as the hours went on. Everything is pristine. There are no weeds sprouting between the tea bushes, and there certainly are not any herbicides or pesticides. Instead, the farmers might use ducks, for instance, to pick the pests off of the bushes and fertilize the soil. I saw firsthand how important the soil conditions in which tea is grown are and what a big role that plays in creating high-quality tea.

Here I also had my first exposure to the many processes tea goes through after the leaves are picked—the baking, rolling, and drawing to bring the juices of the tea up to the surface before it's molded into its final shape. I saw how the different plantations produced different styles and types of tea.

I walked away with an understanding that the reason the tea leaves from this area of the world are so special is not just because of the genesis of the leaves themselves, but also because of the way they're grown, picked, curated, and warmed with such attention and care. The details of that attention and care have been refined and passed along through families over the course of many centuries. This sort of ingrained knowledge and craft simply can't be replicated.

Back in my living room, a world away from the Fujian province, things were starting to happen for my little business. A friend of mine put me in contact with a decision-maker at Wolfgang Puck's restaurants. This was a *huge*, very exciting opportunity. I flew to Las Vegas to meet with my contact. It felt like our meeting went well, but he was noncommittal at the end of it. Over the next few months, I met with him several more times, each time telling him that I was meeting with a few other potential or existing clients in the area. This wasn't true at all—*he* was the potential client, and these trips to Las Vegas were turning into an expensive habit. Like many small business owners (at least at the time), I wanted Wolfgang Puck to believe I was a bigger, more established business than I actually was.

At last, word of my tea trickled down to one of Wolfgang Puck's chefs. He was intrigued and wanted to try it. He loved the tea and started telling other chefs about it. Before you know it, those other chefs got on board too. I was invited to talk to that group of exceptionally high-caliber chefs about the origin of our teas and to share the stories of how they were crafted and hand-blended. These chefs all knew a lot about wine and coffee, but they didn't know a lot about tea and were excited to learn. I loved the opportunity to educate them; it was a true honor. I was also very lucky that they had such a genuine thirst for knowledge. After all, I was new enough that I couldn't sell Art of Tea by pointing to other noteworthy accounts I already had under my belt. I had to sell myself based on my knowledge of and passion for the product, as well as my ability to translate that knowledge in a way that was impactful.

In the end, we made the deal. It felt like winning the lottery, just an incredible rush.

The initial agreement was that Wolfgang Puck would carry Art of Tea in one of their restaurants. We rolled out there, and I trained all of their executive chefs. Then Art of Tea went into three Wolfgang Puck restaurants. At that point, one of the head guys there told me, "Don't fuck this up. If you crush this, we'll be working together for a very long time. I take good care of my people, and if we're in this together, I'll take good care of you too."

Over the years, I've taken a lot of care not to fuck up, and I'm proud to say that Art of Tea has gone on to establish a true, very interactive partnership with Wolfgang Puck. That partnership has been massive for Art of Tea. Over the years, it's opened the door for us to collaborate with a lot of other five-star restaurants, hotels, and spas.

Funnily enough, not long ago, I ran into one of the Wolfgang Puck chefs who was a supporter of mine early on. "Man, I remember you!" he said. "I'm pretty sure you were working out of the back of your car."

I laughed and told him he wasn't too far off.

"I love that!" he replied.

In *Art of War*, Sun Tzu advises to appear strong when you are weak, and weak when you are strong. In the early days of Art of Tea, I'd had all of these beliefs about what potential clients who I considered to be prestigious wanted to see. But really, they were most happy to know that I was going to the farm directly to source my teas. They were happy to see that I could speak intelligently about my blends and train their staff in kind. That's what *actually* mattered to them. Today, now that Art of Tea has found some success, I make a point of focusing on getting great rather than getting big. I want to make sure we always remain curated and specific, both in what we offer and who we work with.

Once this deal with Wolfgang Puck was struck, the real work began. I now had to blend, deliver, pack, and label in bulk. I had to get the right software in place and enter SKUs. And I also had to take care of all the accounting behind this. I quickly learned that a lot of things have to be in place and running smoothly just to get tea into a restaurant.

In addition to managing this big win, I also knew it was time to double down. Most people double down when they're losing, but Brian Tracy, a prominent business speaker and coach, talks about how those moments when you have a big win are actually the time to go hard. Wins bring with them a certain energy that others can pick up on and that they respond to. It's a lot like dating: the person who is the most confident is also usually the person who's the most attractive. That's not a coincidence. Today, my sales team still subscribes to this philosophy.

As the business expanded, my wife understandably grew tired of all of the boxes of tea piling up in our living room. After about twelve months of running Art of Tea from our home, Leetal told me that either I could move out or my boxes could. Luckily (for me, at least), a friend of mine owned a framing business that was not doing well as a result of the economy's downward descent in 2007. He was more than happy to generate some extra income by putting up a wall to create a separate space and renting it to Art of Tea.

Even though I couldn't afford it, and it felt like a big leap, I also knew I had reached the right juncture to bring in a couple of employees. The Wolfgang Puck deal alone took up a lot of bandwidth. Art of Tea was growing and moving in the right direction, but I knew that it couldn't continue to grow without more manpower. I hired according to the strategy author Michael Gerber set forth in his book *The E-Myth*. I wrote out an org chart that included every position or function that Art of Tea required in order to grow. Then I wrote my name next to each function I could do myself. I was left with a couple of things I really sucked at, and those two things directed me to my first hires—two people who loved doing the things I was really bad at.

I know that I shine when it comes to teaching and talking about tea, which had come in very handy when representing the company and selling tea to new clients. But I was so busy packing the tea and doing accounting work (which is *not* my strength) that I was holding the business back by limiting the time I had to blend and sell. So one of those first hires helped with packing, and the other helped with data and accounting. On their first day, Art of Tea officially moved out of my living room and into our new 500-square-foot space. To this day, I still have the picture of the three of us moving boxes hanging in my office.

While I had no business bringing on staff at that point, they lit a fire under me to build Art of Tea. I needed to make sure they got paid, and I needed to get paid too. Not only did this scenario end up working, but it also taught me a valuable lesson about myself as a business leader: if something simultaneously freaks me out and gets me excited, it's a sure sign I'm doing the right thing. But first, I will temper that excitement by taking forty-eight hours to contemplate any decision before moving forward. I allow myself to feel the anxiety that comes with making new moves, and I marinate on the worst-case scenario, the absolute *worst* thing that can happen. I then work backward to figure out what I can do to prevent that worst-case scenario from happening. It's full-steam ahead from there.

At the same time I created that initial org chart in my living room, I also wrote out the twenty-one reasons why I wanted Art of Tea to succeed, a tactic I had learned from Tony Robbins on my honeymoon. For me, the number one reason to succeed was because my wife and I had a baby on the way. I wanted to make sure I created a business and life that allowed me to fully show up for our little family. After creating that list, I went to an office supply store and bought a piece of poster board, then cut out a bunch of images from magazines to remind me why success mattered. That vision board hung on the wall of Art of Tea's office for a long time to serve as a daily reminder of my vision. I came back to that board time and time again when I needed to refocus or double down.

Just a few years into Art of Tea, I was offered a million-dollar buyout. This was a lot of money to me—the business wasn't even doing a million dollars a year at that point. I took the offer to my attorney, who told me, "You're never going to get offered a million dollars in your life. Take the check."

Leetal and I thought long and hard about it. The offer was tempting, but it didn't sit entirely right. The company that had offered to buy me out wanted to use tea as a diet mechanism, and that's not aligned with my purpose. Yes, I want to do well—I want to raise capital and create security for my family—but I also want to do good. I believe these two things can go together, hand in hand. In the end, Leetal and I decided that we were still young and that there was still potential for the business. Why not keep going and see what we could do and how far we could take it?

Ultimately, the business that wanted to buy us out tanked.

Looking back, it's hard to imagine all of the experiences and growth I would have missed had I sold Art of Tea at that early point. There was still so much to do and learn in business, in the craft, and as a teacher.

For as passionate as I am about blending, I have always envisioned myself as a teacher above all else. One of the things I love most about Art of Tea is that it's given me the opportunity to teach about tea at publicly traded companies and to sold-out audiences at worldwide conventions. About three years into Art of Tea, I was approached to teach my first course on blending at an international tea convention. Word got back to us that some of our competitors flipped out about this. They couldn't believe that I was willing to give away the secrets of blending. *What if it saturates the market?* they worried. My philosophy has always been that if you give away 85 percent of your information, you can build a solid foundation of trust with your clientele. From there, the product sells itself.

It turned out that people were interested in learning how to blend tea. First, there were thirty spots available for my lecture, and then, when those filled, the conference organizer pushed it to fifty, then sixty. On the day of the event, people who weren't able to sign up begged me to come into the class anyway. I ended up teaching to a packed house, with as many people squeezed in as possible. The next year, I was booked for both a beginning and an advanced blending course.

After I taught the course for the second year, a guy approached me and introduced himself as David. "Obviously, you know what you're doing," he said. "I own a company, and we're going to make our own teas. Can you formulate them for us?"

That's how Art of Tea came to create the initial formulations for DavidsTea, now a publicly traded tea company. This partnership ended up earning us a lot of street cred and also positioned us as an authority in the blending space. Not only that, but from a business perspective, working with DavidsTea was a great move for us. Art of Tea wasn't in direct competition with DavidsTea since they were a Canadian direct-to-consumer company, while we were primarily B2B. Also, creating their DavidsTea formulations allowed us to purchase our product at greater volume for a lower price per kilo, which allowed Art of Tea to expand.

One of my favorite custom blends is one that we did with Shutters on the Beach, a luxury hotel in Santa Monica with a lot of personality. To create the blend, I asked if Shutters had a signature scent. They gave me a shampoo bottle and asked if I could somehow make it into a tea. Of course, no one wants to drink shampoo (or anything that tastes remotely like it), but I took the high and low notes from the shampoo and created a blend around it. All those years of developing my olfactory senses through Ayurveda and doing breathwork in meditation were coming in very handy now.

When we delivered that first batch of tea to Shutters, we hand-sealed and labeled each and every bag. They ordered fifty cases, so packing it up took us all night. Just a few days later, Shutters called to tell us they loved the tea and wanted to order 150 more cases.

Over the years, Art of Tea has created signature blends for a wide range of clients, including Vera Wang, Slack, Google, Disney, Dita Von Teese, the Getty, LACMA, the Shangri-La Hotel in Tokyo, and the Ritz Carlton. (I'm also happy to say that our packing process has evolved in that time, as well!) Each of these collaborations is unique. I begin by visiting the site and getting a feel for the setting—I want to know about the physical space and the aromas and also to learn more about what a company wants to accomplish with their tea.

One step at a time, Art of Tea has built up its authority, beginning with sourcing, then blending, and then training and teaching. One of my favorite teaching experiences was training the first tea sommelier in the US at Caesars Palace. Up to that point, only one other tea sommelier existed in the world that

I'm aware of, and he was located in London. Once a month, I flew out to Vegas for a couple of days at a time to train her, or alternatively, she came to our office. At the time, we were still in our makeshift office behind my friend's framing business, so the majority of our trainings were conducted on a desk we created out of a door stretched across two file cabinets. She was a great sport and soaked in all of the information we provided her with about origin, tasting, and how to train others. At the end of her training, we created her a certificate from Kinko's.

Over the years, it's been wonderful to watch this woman's career and experience blossom. Today, she teaches her own tea programs, both at Caesars Palace and off-site. Not only has the education and training spread the impact of tea, but it's also raised Art of Tea's visibility. She's no longer the sole tea sommelier in America; today, various high-end hotels and restaurant groups around the country have this service, and we often play a big role in training the sommelier.

While there are other tea companies in America, there are only one or two that do what we do at Art of Tea. Most are essentially marketing companies—they sell teas, but outside producers source, blend, and pack it. Art of Tea is unique insofar as we are vertically integrated. We buy our leaves from growers and take it from there, doing all of our own blending, packing, and distribution. We're a one-stop shop from leaf to cup.

Having said that, one of my driving philosophies is that Art of Tea is not in competition with any other company except for ourselves. When our sales team is asked who our biggest competitors are, they make a point to never speak negatively about another business in our space. The only thing that ultimately accomplishes this is drawing the attention away from what Art of Tea does and creates. Our answer is this: "Our competitor is the status quo." And that's the truth. If Art of Tea can stand among the top 2 percent of teas produced throughout the world (which I believe we do), we're breaking the status quo. Moreover, I believe that all boats rise with the tide. The better quality and value we provide, the more everyone else has to bring their A game as well. Ultimately, that's what I want to see more than anything else in order to ensure that the maximum number of people in this country and world receive the maximum amount of benefits that hand-harvested, hand-picked, artesian tea offers.

Art of Tea grew more quickly than I could have imagined. We outgrew that 500-square foot space after about a year and moved to a larger space in downtown LA. We lasted there for about three years, until we grew beyond that too. Finally, we moved out to Monterey Park, where we remain. Today, there are about twenty-five people on the Art of Tea team, all deeply dedicated to and focused on creating impact through the handcrafted, blended teas we produce. In California, where startups sprout up every day and move to mass scale thanks to venture capitalists and private equity groups, what we've experienced wouldn't be considered fast growth by most. But it has been sustained growth, at about 20 percent per year. That's fine with me because we're in it for the long haul. With that, it's important that we manage our company resources wisely. Also, efficiency is not our main goal because handmade products take time. Just like I did in my living room, to this day, we continue to hand-blend, label, and pack each package of tea we put together. That will never change. Amazingly, we still have the capacity to go through two tons of tea per day.

As Art of Tea grew from a three-person business to a twenty-five-person business with distribution partners in Singapore and Japan and expanded into South America and Europe, I continued to follow that strategy of leaning into my own strengths and bringing on others to lean into the strengths that I lacked. Looking back, I can see the role this sort of organizational structure played in building a purpose-driven organization in which each one of us offers our best and supports everyone else in offering theirs. Every single day, I'm grateful to work with a group of people who take tea and its impact as seriously as I do.

Every single person at Art of Tea is protective of the environment in which we blend because we want to know that our product is infused with harmonious and intentional energy. As we blend, we are specific, considering the way in which taste hits the human tongue and how the tea will be experienced out in the world. Much like the pharmacy at the Ayurvedic Institute, we think of our blending room as a sacred space and carefully consider everything from the room to the music to the directional force in which we blend the teas. We are mindful that our blends include botanicals that are grown all over the world—we bring in a lot of energy this way and also infuse our own energy into it.

Art of Tea has yet to open a brick-and-mortar storefront because, much like I felt practicing Ayurveda on an individual basis didn't create the larger impact I craved, I feel the same is true of a storefront business. By producing and distributing our teas to large companies, and largely building our business on a B2B basis, we're able to multiply the impact of our teas by getting them in front of larger audiences. It's for this reason that training and education are such an important part of what we offer—they're integral to this idea of impact. We train the trainers at our various partners, teaching them our specific methodology and, more generally, how to become tea experts in their own right. We share our knowledge with our partners, and they are, in turn, able to train their own staff on the elements of tea we consider important, such as origin, taste, and benefits. From there, that information trickles down to customers.

Whenever I think about how I want to lead my company, I go back to a conversation I had with my friend Amil many years ago. Not only is Amil a Holocaust survivor, but he was born in a concentration camp. He made it out alive, came to the US with nothing, and is extremely successful today. Shortly after I opened Art of Tea, I had dinner at his house. As always, I was struck by how he maintained such a positive perspective, despite all of the adversity he had to overcome throughout his life.

That night, I decided to ask Amil how he did it. Even as I asked, I felt a sort of guilt about the question because I knew he must be asked the same thing all the time.

Amil sat up straight-backed in his chair, and the crow's feet around his eyes deepened. His face gleamed as he looked at me and smiled. But he said nothing.

Thinking Amil must not have heard me, I asked again, "Amil, how did you do it?"

This time, Amil nodded his head as he continued smiling. I figured that perhaps he was considering his answer or, alternatively, wondering what a little schmuck like me was doing pestering him.

Still, one more time I asked him, "How did you create this?"

Finally, he answered. "Steven," he said in his thick Eastern European accent, "I'm showing you. This is how I did it. It's amazing what you can get done with just a smile."

So often in business, it seems to me that we believe success comes through wielding an iron fist or dominating everyone in our path. We get competitive and fall into the belief that we need to take something from others in order to get what we want or need. I never forgot what Amil showed me that day, which is that there is an abundant amount of success to be had simply through the act of extending kindness. And of course, he's right. Who wants to work with people who aren't clear and kind, positive and optimistic? Certainly not me.

CHAPTER FIVE

NAVIGATING THE UNFORESEEN

Like any business owner, I'm proud of what my company has achieved and the impact we've had so far. But this doesn't mean that the future is certain or that we have all of the answers. As I write this book in 2021, I've spent the past few months being reminded that no matter how much we plan or think to the future, there's always a degree of uncertainty ahead.

As it turns out, sometimes there's a *lot* of uncertainty ahead.

Every single member on my team at Art of Tea takes their job very seriously. Many businesses hire for experience, and sure, that makes sense. But I hire for attitude and ability. I look for a variety of traits, but one of the main characteristics I'm drawn to is tenacity. Are the people I work with tenacious enough to keep our mission in mind even on the days when doing so is difficult?

To me, the phrase "purpose-driven" is much more than a catchphrase. Our team members understand that customers are engaged with our tea in a special, meaningful way, and that flavors the energy of the work we do on every level. I believe that if a business is truly driven by a real, specific purpose such as this, that purpose can act as the driver necessary to navigate even the most difficult, uncertain times.

Thank God for that tenacity and purpose. Over the years, Art of Tea has certainly navigated its fair share of rough terrain, but never anything that put this idea of tenacity and purpose to the test like the COVID-19 crisis.

By the beginning of 2020, things were flying along for us. We were consistently growing in the double-digit percentages. We were landing new accounts both domestically and abroad, including large offices, resorts, hotels, and cruise lines. We had begun to gather some steam in our online direct-to-customer audience too. There's no other way to say it: we were crushing it, and the entire team was rowing in the same direction.

Because of my interaction with Eastern countries, I was one of the few business owners who were able to wrap my head around the severe, all-encompassing impact of COVID-19 before it actually landed on US shores. I spent a significant amount of time speaking with companies that we distribute to in Singapore and Japan because they were about a month ahead of us. They made it clear that the impact of COVID-19 was devastating from a business perspective. Thankfully, there was good news to be had too, though. My Eastern partners were seeing that once the lockdown was over, people craved opportunities to commune and be social. I shared these discussions with my team, and they became our guiding light. We braced for impact and understood that we had to summon up the tenacity to make it to the other side—that there *was* another side.

One of the gifts of living through such uncertainty and scarcity as a child is that I cultivated grit. That grit allowed me to become a hyperrealist. I understand that I have to see reality for exactly what it is at any given moment: no filtration, no judgment, just homing in on the situation at hand so that I can lean in and make quick, intelligent decisions to move myself forward. In this case, I knew that before Art of Tea could get to that light up ahead, we had to feel our way through the dark.

Art of Tea's relatively unique situation allowed us to see further down the highway than most. We could crane our necks to see that the traffic up ahead was at a standstill and let our foot off of the gas rather than slamming on the brakes at the last minute. I called my top vendors and told them what I saw coming because I didn't want them to be caught off guard. I was transparent and communicative with my leadership team about what I thought we should expect and stayed present with how everyone on my team reacted. We immediately reached out to our bank, lines of credit, and utility companies in an attempt to get ahead of the tsunami that was likely coming our way.

Even at that, it was difficult to understand what COVID-19 would really mean in practice. Never did anyone in America anticipate being under stay-at-home orders for months at a time. It was particularly upending in California, which was the first state to close down. Not only that, but because Art of Tea primarily serves the hospitality and B2B sectors, our wheels all but ground to a halt. Almost immediately, our business went down by 80 percent.

I leaned hard on people who are smarter than me, asking for their help in crafting wise decisions as we waded our way through. During this time, I have appreciated more than ever the circle of wise counsel I have surrounded myself with. This consists of six businesspeople who own bigger companies than I do, possess far more wisdom than me, and have way more gray hair. Collectively, they have gone through several cycles of recession and difficult transition. Thanks to them, I was as prepared as possible for what was to come and understood the conversations that needed to be had. I fully understood that Art of Tea could not weather this period if I were to screw my eyes shut, hang on for dear life, and hope that everything was going to work itself out. I knew I had to show up.

Just because I saw what was coming and had a general understanding of what needed to be done doesn't mean Art of Tea was able to avoid pain. We experienced plenty of it. Just a few weeks into lockdown, I had to furlough half of my staff, which was deeply painful. Back in 2008, one of my coaches named Mark Moses put together a list of practices to help companies thrive in a down economy. One of the checkboxes on that list was to cut fast and deep. The logic behind this is that if you only cut a little bit, you'll likely have to keep going back to cut more, which causes a decline in morale. Team members begin to disengage, constantly wondering if they're the next to go.

I desperately wanted to avoid this because culture is nothing short of critical at Art of Tea. I met with my CFO, and together, we figured out how many team members we would have to cut to compensate for the huge drop in sales. I then met with the leadership team, and together, we determined which team members we felt could really drive through and soar with freedom and opportunity. It was also important to me that the remaining staff consisted of team members who could show me where my blind spots were so that I could identify and overcome them throughout these very extenuating circumstances.

It wasn't easy saying goodbye to half of the Art of Tea team (even temporarily), but the idea was that through this finite pain, we could all come out not only intact but also stronger in the long run. Still, I cried as I drove home the evening we broke the news to our staff. I hadn't cried in a long time. Thankfully, because we initially cut so deep, we actually found that we were able to bring some team members back almost immediately once our direct-to-consumer strategy kicked in.

This wasn't the end of the cuts though. I've always followed Richard Branson's advice about training my team members well enough that they can leave but paying them enough that they won't want to. While Art of Tea is certainly not the highest-paying company in Los Angeles compared to tech and entertainment companies, we do pay well and offer a great environment to walk into on a daily basis. And now, this.

I found myself in a position where I had to ask some of my team members to take a salary cut. I had those conversations personally and individually. I began each meeting by letting the team member know how I was cutting back personally in an effort to do everything in my power to ensure we made it through this period. I let them know their salary was not the first place I looked to cut and emphasized how valuable they were as a face of the company, whether that meant sealing packages, answering phones, or providing answers to our customers via online chat. It was only then that I asked if they would be willing to cut X amount of their salary until we made it through COVID-19. I made a point of not giving a solid time frame because there were so many unknowns. Maybe these cuts would last a week, or perhaps it might be a year. There was really no telling, and I wanted to be crystal clear about that.

Each of the remaining staff was laser-focused on making a critical difference so that we could all ultimately survive whatever was to come. We focused deeply on how we could get more efficient with our operations, with the goal of quickly getting to a place where we could bring all of our team members back. I was delighted to see that this goal seemed to instill a sense of deep purpose into everyone who was still a team member. I saw it as my job to keep everyone on board with their eyes on the prize. Not only for the ultimate survival of Art of Tea but also for each person's individual mental and emotional wellness. I'm happy to say that this sense of purpose created even more of a tribal culture than I'd ever seen in my company before. We made a concerted effort to build the survival of Art of Tea upon tactics that directly related back to our core mission. Interestingly, because we made this promise to ourselves, it felt like we collectively moved up Maslow's hierarchy of needs to achieve a sense of purpose rather than slogging around in survival. I suspect we would have been mucking around in survival had our focus remained entirely on financial reports and P&Ls.

Since the hospitality industry wasn't a viable option to build sales, our team realized we had to get creative about leveraging a wider audience if we wanted to continue on. We thought long and hard about the different channels we could reach and places where we could get deeper traction. Where should we put our focus and emphasis now? Where were we best to lean in and fail fast? To stay true to ourselves, we also had to find a solution within these parameters that stayed true to our core value of impact. With each potential solution, we had to ask ourselves two additional questions: *Will this solution impact our customers' lives? Will it impact our business?*

We also knew we had to be smart because we had a limited amount of money to invest with business so far down. We subscribed to *Good to Great* author Jim Collins's theory and realized there were two tactics we could use to fight for our survival: machine gun or single-shot rifle. A machine gun sprays out a bunch of bullets with a single shot. A rifle, on the other hand, shoots out one targeted bullet at a time. In dire situations, many companies default to the machine-gun strategy. They spray at whatever targets are potentially in shooting range and hope to hit something. When it comes to marketing dollars, this is a frantic approach that causes companies to run out of ammo quickly. We opted to take the rifle strategy and aim for a single target demographic: tea drinkers. This was the more low-cost, low-risk approach. For the first time in the history of Art of Tea, we set our sights on a direct-to-consumer audience in a big way and as a primary strategy.

During the period of rapid ideation, anything was fair game. We threw a ton of ideas against the wall to see what stuck. Once we sifted through the plausibility and potential failure points of each idea—no matter how off the wall it might be—we settled on one that seemed to make the most sense, went all in on it, and were prepared to fail fast and draw out quickly if it didn't work.

Since everyone was stuck at home, we decided to launch an online course called Art of Tea Academy. The in-depth program included twenty-five modules of in-depth content and videos about the history of tea, the how-tos of tea, and so much more. This strategy was aligned with my philosophy that if you give away 85 percent of your information, people will buy the additional 15 percent. The best way to earn people's trust is to build their knowledge by sharing your own. This tactic also aligned with Art of Tea's emphasis on giving and contribution, which felt important. We launched the course for free for the first ninety days and then increased the price to twenty dollars. The minimal price point was for the energy exchange and also because studies show that people value a paid purchase more than a complimentary gift.

Thankfully, there was some synchronicity at play. Right before the pandemic hit, Art of Tea was getting ready to launch a new website. As part of this, we had taken a slew of video footage six months before. The filming was complete, although the editing and site development weren't slated to take place for some time.

Prior to the pandemic, we had already invested a significant amount of money in the planned site refresh. However, the decision to edit the videos, create a learning platform, and kick the site live was still a difficult decision to make. It required us to invest more money earlier than we had anticipated doing so and, certainly, in a situation we hadn't foreseen. In times of economic strife, the tendency is to hold back on launches and cease investments. There's no doubt about it: this was a big investment for us to make during a critically low point. After a lot of discussion, we decided to take the risk and lean in. Not only would the new site allow us to educate online, but it would also streamline our operations, provide a more efficient online shopping experience, and provide us with better insights and engagement, which would allow us to create more impact.

We went into this endeavor well aware that we might fail, but if that turned out to be the case, we wanted to fail quickly. We believed there was the potential to use this moment in time as an opportunity to establish Art of Tea as leaders in the tea space by contributing to the average person's knowledge about tea. We figured that since they were stuck at home, people would be more apt to dive into topics they had always been curious about but never had time to invest in. This seemed like it could be particularly true when it came to tea—a beverage that offers so many health benefits—in this time when wellness and immunity were more pressing than ever before. There is also the fact that tea is an item of comfort, and comfort was suddenly critical. We were also aware that consumers who did still have gainful employment during the pandemic were being extremely mindful about how they could contribute to the economy and that many of them were supporting independent businesses like Art of Tea.

When the new site and educational program launched, we got a lot of direct feedback from customers about what was wrong and what needed to be fixed. We went into the launch with a long, established history of thanking our customers for feedback—especially harsh and critical feedback—so it turns out we had set ourselves up nicely for this scenario. Our customers are always our teachers, and in this case, that was truer than ever before. They provided us with the opportunity to quickly identify and fix things that weren't working or needed to be smoothed out. For example, our shopping cart solution was broken when we went live. That's no good for any business, but let me tell you, tea drinkers are very passionate about their tea, and they want what they want when they want it. Especially during uncertain and uncomfortable times like these. Since our remaining team members were all leaning in together, what could have felt like big stumbling blocks instead seemed manageable. We fell, but we got up quickly. This was critical because had we gotten stuck on the things that went wrong, we would've been screwed.

I'm not going to lie. The sprint to launch and then the immediately ensuing sprint to fix what was broken was exhausting. During those weeks, I often thought back to an experience I'd had in Israel. One day when I was teaching students horticulture, I was feeling lazy and lethargic, so I went to grab some coffee in the teacher's lounge. As I was pouring my coffee, a fellow teacher who was always bright and energetic walked in. As usual, she had a glow to her.

"How are you doing?" she asked me.

"I'm tired," I replied.

"You know," she said, "the more energy you give, the more you get."

That simple comment was a wake-up call. *Am I really giving enough?* I wondered at that moment. *Am I really putting enough into this?* I have continued to ask myself those same questions throughout the duration of my life. And I certainly asked them of myself on a near hourly basis as Art of Tea battled back against the fallout of COVID-19.

Along with the bigger strategic moves Art of Tea made, we also made smaller ones, such as offering remote worker relief kits for our corporate clients, such as Google, to send to their staff. In some instances, we got really creative with this. For instance, we partnered with Nike to host a remote tasting for their team members. Employees in their creative division were sent a box of tea samples, and then we all logged on to a Zoom call to walk Nike's staff through the flavors, benefits, and experience of their teas.

We made a point of weaving in a structure for giving back too. For every ten boxes of tea a company purchased, Art of Tea donated an additional box to a first responder from an ambulance company in Southern California. With this, we asked our social media followers to nominate a first responder on a weekly basis. We received and shared stories, then invited our followers to vote for the recipient. The entire process was incredibly heartwarming, and it fed our team, serving as a constant reminder of our greater purpose. We created a board in our offices where we shared feedback from customers about this program so that every day our team members could walk by and experience a quick reminder of how their work was positively impacting people's lives. It reminded us that we are putting more out into the world than just leaves with a label. There's a greater purpose, even if that purpose is at times intangible.

One of the more obvious tactics we could have taken during the pandemic was to slant our marketing toward the antiviral quality of tea. After all, there's plenty of support for this, not only in Ayurveda, but also in the world of Western medicine. Specifically, studies have shown that black and green teas help fight SARs, which is in the same family as COVID-19. In the end, though, we decided this wasn't the route for us. While I'm drawn to the health benefits of tea, the ultimate impact I want to provide through Art of Tea is an experience that's both calming and delicious. Bringing in antiviral messaging—particularly during this moment in history—is anything but calming. Also, I know from Ayurveda that there isn't necessarily a single solution for everyone's experience of the same issue. For example, there are so many different ways to experience a headache: it might be a dull, sharp, shooting, piercing, or burning sensation. The solutions for each of those symptoms is different. This is to say that I didn't want Art of Tea to make promises we couldn't ultimately keep, even if I do generally believe there is great benefit to drinking specific types of tea for overall wellness. During any time—but especially during times like the pandemic—I never want to do anything for the sake of clicks alone.

I thought through all of this painstakingly. Just as much as it was important to me that Art of Tea stayed true to who we are during this crisis, it was also important to me that I remain true to the values I've always held as a leader. In Japan, business leaders think out each decision three generations forward. Sure, I may very well not be the leader of Art of Tea even thirty years from now, but it still feels important for me to make sound decisions with the long run in mind.

Throughout these trying times, I focused a lot on my own behavior and how I was showing up as a leader. This included everything from my messaging to my physical presence. In this time, more than any other, it felt as if my main role was to coach, mentor, and guide employees so they could bring out their personal best. I was diligent about monitoring our team members and made sure my channels of communication with them remained as open, transparent, and honest as possible. Every day, I asked a few basic questions of each team member: "How are you doing? What are you working on today? What's in your way?" These three simple questions served me so well because they allowed team members the opportunity to share what was happening from their perspective.

Beyond that, I made sure to stay in the loop with how everyone's families were doing. Each person on my team handled the pandemic differently. I noticed that one team member was literally holding her breath all of the time. I gently pointed that out and walked her through some breathwork exercises, a weekly digital detox, and talked a lot about focusing on well-being. Meanwhile, other team members were really getting in the zone. Wherever a team member fell along the spectrum, I considered my understanding of their state to be my most important job. Many mornings, I woke up at five o' clock to get some of my own work out of the way before going into the socially distanced office, just so that I could be sure I had the time and space available to be really present, really *there* with my staff. This is always important, but never is it more important than in trying times. In my opinion, a boss who hides out or becomes hyperfocused on business rather than people in moments like these is signing up for near-certain doom.

Beyond supporting the business and my team, I also felt it was important to contribute to other businesses that might be struggling. The way I saw it, there were going to be three types of companies at the end of all of this: companies who were not going to come back at all, companies who were barely going to scrape by, and companies who were going to emerge thriving. Every single business around was figuring out how to navigate the odds on the fly, and it made sense to me that we would information-share as we learned through trial and error.

We tasked our sales and customer service teams to start calling our partners who were still open for business in an attempt to create a network of sorts. We asked our partners what they were doing to stay alive and what, if anything, Art of Tea could do to help them along the way. How could we show up for them? When I came upon a company that was thriving, we asked if it was okay to share some of their strategies with other companies in our network so that we could all learn together. As a result, Art of Tea became a conduit through which various restaurants and cafés that were struggling could learn and spark their own creativity. It was a very cool experience to see businesses coming together as allies.

The unchartered waters of the pandemic also offered an opportunity to create alliances with other companies and organizations that might not have happened otherwise. For example, COVID-19 ended up pushing forward a partnership that we had been in discussion with the Try Guys about for more than a year. The Try Guys do exactly what it sounds like they do—they try different things and share that experience with their 7.5 million followers. From this has grown a business of products, including a hot sauce that resulted from their challenge to a vendor to come up with a new hot sauce concept. The Try Guys decided they wanted to build upon that success and bring a tea to market in much the same way. Prior to the pandemic, they contacted Art of Tea about a licensing deal to make that happen.

The pandemic pushed things forward. Together, we created a series of six videos that were extremely fun to film. We were elated because many of the Try Guys' followers fall into a younger demographic than ours, so it allowed Art of Tea to create a meaningful touchpoint with a younger generation in a way that is fun, dynamic, and engaging.

I love this idea of cross-collaboration, and I think we're going to see a lot more of it as businesses look for ways to lift themselves out of the economic uncertainty. Synergistic relationships can appeal to new audiences and breathe new life and creativity into the partners involved. It can shake them out of their typical ways of thinking and interacting. In my opinion, this has been Apple's secret sauce for a long time, dating back to when they opened up their app platform for free when the iPhone launched. I believe the synergy it's created is a large part of the reason why Apple continues to dominate. Of course, it's also important to be thoughtful when it comes to collaboration. Part of finding the right synergy is saying no to a lot of the opportunities and homing in on those that will have the biggest impact and that are most aligned with your company.

It seems to me that one of the results of the COVID-19 pandemic was a collective waking up. This, of course, means different things to different people. For me, it promoted an energy of scrappy creativity and an even greater sense of purpose. During the lockdown, it felt like so much was (necessarily) put on pause—but creativity was one of the few things that were still on the table. The physical confines on daily life created a new opportunity to create, innovate, and strategize, and this has applied equally to everyone at Art of Tea, including functions that are typically seen as less creative, such as sales. It's forced people to think about how to be creative without throwing money at a solution. I believe there's also a lot to be said for being in your own home, hopefully a safe space and cocoon, and figuring out how to make an impact from there.

Having said all of that, none of this means there wasn't fear. Hell yes, there was fear. I still feel fear as I write this book. From a business perspective (and many other perspectives, as well), we're currently living through the great unknown. We don't know what the waves headed in our direction look like, and this is intrinsically a situation in which constant adjustment and reevaluation are necessary. I'm relentlessly trying to leverage that fear as a driver for optimization. Being a born optimist helps.

While I will never be glad that a pandemic occurred, I do think that there's a sort of beauty to what it's done on a business level. (I say this recognizing, of course, that there are plenty of businesses that have suffered greatly and left people in dire straits—so many lives around the world that have been adversely affected by this horrible virus). It reminds me of something that happens in California a lot: huge forests are destroyed, sometimes totally obliterated, in wildfires. On the one hand, it's tragic to see so much majestic beauty burned to the ground. But over the long term, rejuvenated, healthier soil and new growth emerge. From destruction arises new, cleaner, healthier, flourishing life. I believe that COVID-19 is causing a similar effect in business. So much is being burned to the ground, and the destruction is painful and feels out of control. I suspect, though, that out of this, we will ultimately see new, healthier growth and flourishing over the long run. I think that in the next eighteen months to three years we will see a better-constructed society with healthier ways of living. It's my goal to help guide Art of Tea to that place.

While COVID-19 has certainly been an extenuating circumstance, like any other company that wants to make it over the long haul, Art of Tea has to continue to move forward and innovate. We have to continue to be fresh and dynamic in our ideas, blends, and sources to remain relevant. Even though tea itself is ancient, business principles still apply. Navigating our way through COVID-19 has been a reminder of that. Even when this is all said and done, we'll continue to push the envelope—and sometimes, we'll fuck up. In my mind, it's all about firing those single, targeted shots until we feel like we've nailed the bull's-eye. Then we start launching cannonballs at that bull's-eye. That's when things really start to move forward in a big way.

Now more than ever, I'm aware that, like every other business, Art of Tea will see high points as a company, and we'll see low points as well. But as long as our North Star is clear and everyone is rowing in the same direction, we'll be able to weather whatever storms come our way. I do believe that, as is the case for so many other businesses, COVID-19 has represented a defining moment for Art of Tea. My hope is that the company will exist long beyond my time on this planet and that whatever we learn from this experience can be applied for future generations to come.

Thank you for joining me in my journey with tea. Now let's talk about *your* tea journey.

PART TWO

UNDERSTANDING THE ART OF TEA

CHAPTER SIX

LET'S TALK
ABOUT TEA

Believe it or not, tea is actually a technology disruptor. Yes, you read that right.

Tea first disrupted technology about five thousand years ago when it appeared on the scene as the first energy drink—way before Monster or Red Bull. The origin story goes like this: there was a Zen Buddhist monk, who also happened to be an emperor and a poet. He liked to boil water as part of his daily ritual and always left it on the windowsill to cool for a little while before drinking. As luck would have it, one day, as the water was cooling on the windowsill, a wind picked up and blew a tea leaf (more technically known as *Camellia sinensis*) off of a bush and into the monk's boiling water. Not wanting to waste the water, the monk decided to drink it anyway. Lo and behold, he felt an incredible surge of rejuvenation, energy, and inspiration. This monk started to proclaim the drink's healing benefits.

All these thousands of years later, people still draw the correlation between tea and inspiration. Have you ever heard the phrase "tea mind"? Ask a tea drinker, and they will tell you it's a thing. Tea simultaneously enlivens us while also allowing us to focus. Think about it: Could you imagine sitting in a state of inspiration with three shots of espresso in you? That would be really difficult for most of us.

This tea mind was seen as so valuable in earlier Eastern societies that it was utilized by Japanese armies. Samurai warriors ground up tea leaves into matcha and carried that matcha with them in a little pouch. Before they engaged in battle, the samurais added water to the leaves and drank the matcha. With that drink, they felt empowered and ready for battle.

The esteemed place of tea in Eastern warfare went even further than this. Imagine if you will two groups of samurais, representing two different sides of a battle. Now envision a little tent between those two groups. In that tent are two generals, who sit across from one another at a small table with two chairs. Tea is set out before them. One general pours the tea, while the other lifts the cup and sips.

Through this simple yet meaningful interaction, the generals come to an unspoken understanding about which side has lost a war. The generals were able to make this determination based on the minute mannerisms in pouring and sipping. Which general was nervous and which one was confident? Confidence won the war, and when that confidence was displayed through this tea ceremony, the battle came to an end. No words were spoken, the war ended simply through this act of pouring and drinking the tea. Once the generals stepped out of the tent, one of them would signal to his army that they had won the war; the other would signal that they had lost.

Tea played other roles in earlier Eastern society as well. Just like we now exchange money for goods, people once traded tea for goods. Tea was considered to be valuable, *and* it could be stored over a long period of time. Thousands of years ago, the international distribution chain wasn't exactly what it is today. Back then, the main delivery systems were comprised of camels, who first carried the teas out of the monasteries and throughout Asia to the warriors, royalty, and upper classes who could afford it. As it spread to the greater population in Asia, tea came to be so valued that it was utilized as a form of commerce—in fact, it *transformed* commerce.

Because of the high cost of tea, only royalty could afford to purchase it for the most part. They would then keep the tea in a little box and pull it out for special occasions. The royals would brew a single batch of tea leaves seven to ten times, then give it to their servants to use. Oftentimes, the servants would use the tea a few times themselves, then sell it back to the marketplace. At this point, rich merchants would buy the used tea from the marketplace without knowing it had already been used. In other words, tea circulated, much like currency does today.

Eventually, tea made its way out of the Orient and into Europe, which required a very long trip that took months and months. Originally, the tea leaves were green, but over time, as the merchants stopped and lit campfires every night along the way, the leaves turned black thanks to the combination of time and smoke. Because of this, Europeans thought of tea as a smoky elixir.

Over time, increased sea navigation allowed tea to travel to other continents more expediently. By the 1400s, the demand for tea was so great that chests were packed full of tea leaves and stowed away for sale in foreign lands. At auction, these chests of tea might go for the equivalent of hundreds of thousands of dollars today.

The dawn of clipper ships in the mid-1800s resulted in a huge boon for tea because the ships were so speedy. Rather than taking months to get from Asia to Europe by camel, tea could now make its way from origin to Europe in mere weeks. There was a lot of money to be made in that endeavor and a lot of incentive for being quick about it because the first ships to arrive were always going to make the largest amount of money.

When European merchants first bought tea from clipper ships, they were shocked. Tea, as they had always known it, was black. What were these green leaves? At the time, the Chinese were very keen on keeping their secrets, so they told these European merchants that the leaves on these clipper ships were from green tea plants rather than black tea plants. To this day, many people still think that green and black teas come from two different plants when, in fact, they don't. All tea comes from the same plant, *Camellia sinensis*. The different varietals (green, black, white, oolong, and pu-erh) simply have to do with the way in which the leaves are heated and oxygenated. But more on that in the next chapter.

SOURCING TEA

How often do you stop to think about where the leaves in your tea bag or canister came from? By now, it probably doesn't surprise you to hear that I think about the origin of tea a lot. I find these origin stories fascinating, and one of the great joys of my job is traveling to farms throughout the world to source the most delicious leaves possible.

China is the birthplace of tea. Today, China, India, Japan, Sri Lanka, and Taiwan are considered the five traditional countries of origin for tea. This explains why tea has been embedded into Eastern cultures in a way that it hasn't been in the West. Although tea is grown in some other places, it's these original five countries that really set the bar for what tea can—and, in my mind, *should* be. After all, they've had a lot of practice.

It's important to me that Art of Tea uses the best ingredients as the basis for our blends, and I've now spent a large portion of my life traveling to identify those ingredients at their point of origin. Sometimes my sourcing trips are as short as a few hundred miles north, where some of the best spearmint and peppermint to be found are available along the California and Oregon coasts. But more often than not, my travels take me to the East, where small growers have been perfecting their craft for millennia. These travels have been some of the most revelatory, transcendent, and fulfilling experiences of my life.

I could fill an entire book with stories of my sourcing travels and adventures. I want to share just a couple of anecdotes to illustrate what sourcing entails, how we select producers, and how deeply entrenched tea is in the culture and lives of some of the suppliers Art of Tea is lucky enough to work with.

A few years ago, Art of Tea was one of four tea companies from around the world invited by the government of Japan to spend two weeks meeting with growers, producers, and officials. The intent of this gathering was to provide international tea companies with a better understanding of the Japanese green-tea growing and production process.

Although I already knew quite a bit about tea by that point, I was shocked by how much I *didn't* really understand about what really goes into growing and producing the green teas Japan is so famous for—the soil conditions, different varietals, and even how the flowers are pulled apart from the stem. For example, Japanese growers will plant their tea next to volcanos or use crab shells in the soil because the calcium, minerals, and other nutrients create more flavor and a full mouthfeel. They work hard and utilize generational tactics to ensure their tea leaves are strong enough to withstand the elements yet delicate enough to deliver an amazing taste experience. As it turns out, tea is a lot like people. Teas that are able to endure more hardship (in this case, cold weather) ultimately deliver a more diverse flavor experience. It's sort of like how some of the most interesting people you'll encounter are the ones who have been through challenging times.

Visiting the Japanese establishments where these teas were produced was astounding. The producers took their craft so seriously and had such abundantly clear pride in their teas that even the men who swept the floors wore impeccable suits as they worked. I met one gentleman in particular who had been standing at the same station, doing the same procedure for thirty years. The way in which he manipulated tea leaves into longitudinal shapes was almost lyrical, and the level of craftsmanship and pride he displayed was utterly unparalleled. Even more astounding is that this gentleman would never call himself a master of the craft. In the view of cultures such as this one that have dedicated their lives to tea for generation upon generation, there is still much room for opportunity and improvement.

As part of this particular trip, I attended a government-hosted multiday auction that worked sort of like speed dating. I sat at a table as a myriad of tea growers and producers (often accompanied by a translator) came in for twenty minutes at a time with their tea in hand for people like me to taste. The days were long and intense, and after a while, one tea became indistinguishable from the next. I felt overwhelmed by the notion of finding the absolute best leaves amidst this sort of volume.

Toward the end of the day, a producer stepped into the room with his interpreter. As he prepared the tea, he seemed incredibly nervous, to the point where he was visibly shaking. I didn't know what to expect, and I was stunned when I sipped the tea. It was far and away the best green tea I have ever tasted in my entire life. It was the epitome of *umami*, a word derived from Japanese culture that refers to the ultimate taste with just the right balance of saltiness, sweetness, and astringency. (Umami, by the way, was initially discovered by scientists in two things: seaweed and high-quality Japanese green tea.) As I sipped, the gentleman continued to sweat next to me.

I turned to his interpreter and said, "If you don't mind me asking, why is he so nervous? This is literally the best green tea I've ever had."

Over the years, I've come to learn that Japanese producers often bring translators into the room with them even when they speak English. Usually, this is because they're so meticulous in every way that they fear they'll mispronounce certain words. It was clear that this producer, who I came to learn was named Takashi, fell into this camp. The moment I complimented his tea, Takashi's shoulders visibly relaxed.

Nonetheless, it was the interpreter who replied. It was only through his response that I learned Takashi had recently won an award for not only the best green tea in Kyoto, but the best green tea in all of Japan.

Astounded, I asked, "Then why is he so concerned about whether or not *I* like it?" But to Takashi, who cared about his craft so deeply and intensely, it was important that *everyone* liked his tea, regardless of who they happened to be.

Takashi and I have been working together ever since.

The next year, I went to visit Takashi. He showed me one farm way up in the Uji Mountains in Kyoto that was owned by a farmer he sourced leaves from. That farmer grew a special varietal of the *Camelia sinensis* plant called *goku*, a type of green tea with a grassy, sweet cream profile that is rare and sought after. Goku is often used in matcha, gyokuro, and sencha teas. The farmer had previously found success in the corporate world but, by his early thirties, decided that such a lifestyle wasn't for him. So off he went, far up into the mountains to grow tea. Ten years in, his tea won both bronze and silver awards. That wasn't good enough for him, though, so he literally destroyed all of his plants and started over again from scratch. About seven years later—nearly twenty years after he established the farm—he felt satisfied that he'd gotten it right.

After showing me the beautifully kept bread-loaf-shaped tea fields neatly lined up in rows facing the optimal light of the sun, Takashi and I went back to his house, where he produced his teas using wood tools to steam, bake, and roll the leaves. The composition of these tools is important because the wood allows the leaves to bend and breathe as they heat. As we sat in his yard surrounded by beautiful wooded mountains, Takashi explained that his family had been producing tea for at least ten generations—and perhaps more. But those ten generations were documented.

Takashi has two daughters, and as the father of daughters myself, I was curious about how he viewed the future of this family business. The tea industry in Japan is known for being male-dominated. Takashi responded that he was very excited for his girls to take over the family business so that they could change and lead the next generation. I admire Takashi for many reasons, including his simultaneous reverence for the past and vision for the future.

On another trip, I met up with my old friend and trusted guide Alex (from my first sourcing trip to China) to visit the Fujian province and Wuyi Mountain region. This was an exceptionally exciting trip because the area is located in a secluded mountain region where no one is allowed to go unless they're invited by a producer or someone else who lives there. We had to pass through gates to even enter the region, and from there, it took several days of nauseating driving along dirt roads deep in the bamboo forests, far removed from city pollution and smog, and eating street food to get deep, deep into the mountains where we were headed.

In the end, it was worth every moment of car sickness. Once we arrived, Alex and I were greeted by the sight of beautiful long oolong and black teas grown out of rocks. Much like the best wine comes from tough conditions in which mineral content is high, the same is true with tea. This particular varietal was grown out of volcanic rocks in a secluded area. People are only allowed to make the trek up to the plantations to purchase their teas during one month out of the year: July. Other than that, the area is completely cordoned off. I was fortunate enough to be allowed to visit in the spring for the first flush harvest season to witness the picking and roasting of oolongs like Da Hong Pao and delicious Mao Fang black teas.

It was incredible to have access to and see how these families produced their teas. Many of their houses were raised up on clay brick platforms. Underneath the houses were structures that looked like wood pizza ovens, designed for heating and roasting the tea leaves. After the leaves are roasted, they're massaged and rolled to bring all of the juices up to the surface of the leaf. These teas sell for an extremely high price, as much as thirty dollars per cup. In my opinion, it's worth every penny because these teas are beautifully dynamic and unlike anything I've ever tried. It's been a huge honor for Art of Tea to source them.

On that same trip, I was also lucky to spend time with a tea master named Mr. Bei and to really learn the craft from leaf harvest to cup from one of the greats. Mr. Bei is the tea master of a fair-trade estate in South China. This estate doesn't have a central garden; instead, it has various lots dotted across its campus. Each lot is close to a small production facility or satellite, where the teas are quickly dried to prevent oxidization. This is done as a cooperative effort, with many of the villagers putting their strength to work so that Mr. Bei can craft fine teas. According to Mr. Bei, there are only fourteen harvest days each year at this facility for high-quality white and green teas. Depending upon the weather conditions, the remaining crops can be made into black teas.

The year I visited, the rains came late and were followed by cold weather, which caused the production to drop by 60 percent compared to previous years. That meant a price increase and a waiting game to bid. This is where relationships and cooperation on many levels comes in to ensure fair prices and wages for great quality products.

Each year, Art of Tea has found our groove a little bit more when it comes to sourcing (and having access to) the best products. Using the best practices to obtain these products in a fair, equitable way is also very important to us. From its inception, Art of Tea has worked with organic products, but about four years into the company, we decided we wanted to source directly from growers rather than through third-party companies that verify organic and ethically sourced practices. I planned another trip to Asia with the intent of visiting some of the ethically sourced and organic farms to get a better handle on how they worked. At that point, China had just begun opening up its borders to more distributors in the US, which allowed me to see what was happening behind the scenes in a way that I hadn't before. For me, this trip was about altruism. I wanted to see if it really existed. I wanted to see how (and if) our customers were impacting the lives of tea growers and their children. Were we *really* making a net positive impact in practice, or was it just a nice idea we bought into that made us feel good?

I arrived in Guangzhou and then headed off to visit various tea-growing provinces in Fujian. Once again, Alex served as my guide. In Fujian, I found a great yin and yang of wealth in the small towns and villages where the tea plantations and other agriculture were. It wasn't atypical to see an old woman wheeling along a two-wheeled wooden platform laden with produce while a guy in a Lamborghini whizzed past her. It was a land of extremes—both extreme wealth and extreme poverty.

We started off at the tea markets, which weren't as big or expansive as they had been in Beijing, but these felt more wholesale oriented. As we walked through the market, I noticed how beautifully the teas were laid out. I was particularly interested in the white teas, which we were starting to sell a lot of in the US. At the time, they were becoming known for their health benefits, which include increasing collagen in the skin, fighting prostate and colon cancer, and heart disease. Not only this, but white tea has a delicate taste and feel in the mouth, which meant that the high-end restaurants we worked with were particularly intrigued by white tea varietals.

That year, it just so happened that there was a drought in Fujian, which is the original source for high-quality white teas. In response, the tea farmers who still had to make a living went further into the forests and further out into the fields to find old tea fields that had been abandoned or forgotten. There, in those remote areas where the roots were not so shallow, they found trees that had not only survived but had grown at tremendous speed and to tremendous heights because the leaves had been left to grow unencumbered.

Because of the circumstances in which this tea was cultivated, it was different than any variety of white tea I'd ever seen before. White tea is made of an unopened silver needle bud, which is a series of leaves that are tightly closed. Usually, those leaves are straight, but these were slightly curled and had more of an outer covering, or *hao*, than most white tea leaves. The hao is where all of the antioxidants and amino acids live in white tea, and it's what gives the tea its beautiful silvery shine.

I got to taste this white tea, and it was gorgeous, just phenomenal. When the leaves were brewed, they opened up and revealed a dynamic, natural fragrance and a full, soft mouthfeel. I asked if I could name the leaves, and they said I could. I called it Wild Honey Sprout. I was so enamored by these leaves that I brought the tea back on the plane with me. Wild Honey Sprout was the first really interesting tea Art of Tea was able to source directly. Since then, we have continued to source rare and unique finds like this that just don't exist in the US.

After several days of intense travel, Alex and I headed back to Guangzhou. We flew to the Wuyi Mountain region, and then we drove and drove and drove on a dirt road for several days. We drove higher and higher up the mountain and deeper and deeper into the villages. One day, we stopped at a little restaurant in a forest, where we were asked if we'd like some tea. Of course, we said yes. The server brought us osmanthus, a flower that has a peach-like flavor and is used in a lot of perfumes and flavors. It's incredibly sweet and potent.

I had never seen anything like this osmanthus. It looked...old. Alex translated my comment—which was simply an observation, not a judgment—to the staff. They were horrified. The next thing I knew, about six people had hauled a big sheet into the restaurant. Next came a ten-foot-long branch, which they set on the sheet. And then, right in front of Alex and me, about six people started harvesting fresh osmanthus blossoms off the branch.

For the life of me, I could not figure out what was happening. Then, a few minutes later, they brought some blossoms over to our table and asked if they could serve them to us. I was stunned. To this day, it stands out as one of the most incredible experiences I've ever had. Drinking the fresh nectar from the flowers made me realize how important quality control and proper storing are when it comes to teas and botanicals. In that moment, I decided to increase Art of Tea's efforts to facilitate the best tea storage methods possible to prevent aromatic cross-contamination and deliver to our customers the freshest and most delicious tea experience each and every time.

The more I explored there, the more I understood that working with organic certifiers in China was tricky because their regulations for certification are not the same as in the US, largely for administrative reasons. We had to jump through multiple hoops to get estates to meet our standards so that we could confidently sell their tea as certified organic. It can be a painstaking process, but to me, it's also incredibly worthwhile. Sourcing the best tea leaves (that also happen to be certified organic) is like finding a needle in a haystack, so doing what it takes to procure them always results in a huge sense of victory.

Also on that trip, we visited with a woman who acted as a sort of mayor for an area that included about three hundred farmers who were just starting to incorporate direct trade and ethical sourcing. I was taken by the fact that a woman was giving all of these farmers guidance and direction on best practices because Asia is generally so male-dominated. The way it worked in that area is similar to how the fair-trade system works in much of China: people pick the leaves and weigh them out, then the processor (the people who complete the roasting and drying processes) pay the growers based on that weight.

I watched the entire process unfold. Generally speaking, women head out to the fields to harvest and pick leaves in the late morning after the fog starts to roll off. They put their leaves in large baskets that hang from their backs. It is arduous work, yet there they were singing and embracing the experience. I then watched as the processors steamed, baked, and rolled the leaves. The fragrance was heady and intoxicating—it reminded me of lilacs and grape blossoms.

After I witnessed this, the mayor invited me to come with her to visit the schools and factories to see how fair trade benefited the towns and villages in practice. As we visited the schools and factories and walked throughout the town, I saw the results of direct trade and ethical sourcing. Unlike many other areas I had traveled through in China to this point, the roads in this town were paved and lit. The schools were being developed. The real impact direct trade and ethical sourcing had on the community was incredibly clear. The mayor explained that these improvements were what people like me were paying extra for. As the money came in, the local auditor determined how these funds would be distributed: schools, roads, ambulances, cultural centers, or even weddings (in this culture, setting a new couple off on the right course is considered helpful and important), among many other options.

In my opinion, today, fair trade has become more political than it was back then, to the point where we now buy direct from farmers and pay them equitably as an ethical best practice. I was repeatedly told that fair-trade money went to local officials rather than directly to the growers and producers. This meant that transparency in allocating the funds was often missing. We spoke with farmers and producers to find out what the impact would look like if we could pay more directly, and that idea generated a lot of enthusiasm. Art of Tea went on to take that route, and now the growers we work with can use the money as they see fit. But back then, fair trade worked to a large degree, and I clearly saw the results of it with my own eyes.

Even in the days when fair trade worked, though, it was still imperfect. In addition to potential issues with transparency, in order to even participate in fair trade, the farmers needed to be in a position where they weren't suffering to begin with. To participate, a co-op or program had to be big and profitable enough to participate in the fees associated with fair trade. This meant that many of the smaller farms that needed money the most were discounted from the program altogether.

There were issues with organic farming too. Just like there was a barrier to entry for fair trade, there were financial barriers to being certified as an organic farm as well. Some of the farmers couldn't afford to be part of the organic certifying body, regardless of how organic their practices were. This meant their teas weren't technically considered organic despite the fact that the farmers were so poor they didn't even know what pesticides were—much less use them. That's why today, Art of Tea works with some farmers who are not certified as organic, even though their practices are. We don't advertise these products as organic because they are not technically certified. But we do know that they are in the purest state possible. It feels like the best way to get the products we believe in while also ensuring that money is distributed where it's needed the most.

THE DISRUPTION CONTINUES

Today, some of Art of Tea's biggest clients are the great disruptors of our time. Google and Slack, for instance, both love providing their team with our tea. Both of these companies' livelihoods are dependent on their employees' ability to be creative and fast-moving. Don't get me wrong, I love coffee, and I absolutely drink it. But it's challenging to sit around drinking coffee all day while still remaining creative and nimble. Coffee hits the body differently than tea does, and it tends to result in a jittery, anxious sensation. That amped state makes it more difficult to be intentional in thinking and work. Tea helps a person get in the right frame of mind to focus deeply and creatively. And at the same time, certain types of tea can also relax the body and mind into a calm, meditative state. It's for this reason that tea is used in Zen monasteries throughout Japan as a tool to help with focus while sitting in meditation for long periods of time. I'm sure you can imagine how this would be difficult to do with several shots of espresso.

There's a scientific reason behind this: while coffee is a muscular stimulant, tea stimulates the thyroid, which controls immunity, governance, and metabolism. A couple of shots of espresso will leave a person feeling foggy. Tea, instead, offers a mental clarity that allows for simultaneous sharpness and calm because tea is an adaptogen. Adaptogens have the ability to adapt to the mental frame of mind that the person who is consuming them wants to be in. Tea also contains L-theanine, an amino acid unique to tea that is known to have that chilled-out, happy, destressed vibe that we associate with calm energy.

The majority of the human brain is built to help us survive, with the exception of the very thin cerebral cortex. That part of the brain is designed for future thinking and higher levels of development. Tea can help us get into that particular zone of our brains. It can help us to continue to rise up, to be hyperrealistic in the moment, and also to think through the future. This is particularly true of certain strains of tea, such as Japanese green teas, which have higher polyphenols, contain micronutrients that are packed with antioxidants, and offer potential health benefits.

There are so many other benefits too. Anecdotally, one of the interpreters I traveled through Japan with used to make a practice of shaking hands with others to determine whether or not they were green tea drinkers. In her experience, those who regularly drank green tea generally had softer hands. This test bore out time and time again. I suspect this is because Japanese teas have more particles of amino acids and other vital factors per cup since they are gently steamed. This positively impacts collagen and stimulates metabolism and the immune system.

RITUAL

For all of the disruption that tea has caused over thousands of years, the thing I love most is that it's an age-old tradition. While this ritual looks different in different areas of the world, the common theme is that teatime is a time to slow down. In Morocco, that ritual includes taking a cube of sugar between the teeth and allowing it to slowly melt as the tea is drunk. In Japan, tea drinkers might enjoy a bit of whiskey in their matcha, while in China, they perform a gong fu ceremony in preparation. Even with these differences, the common thread across cultures is carving out some moments of time in which to be mindful and present.

One of the best parts of my job is getting to witness some of these traditional rituals firsthand. When Alex and I were on one of our sourcing adventures in search of an oolong tea called Ti Kuan Yin, also known as the Iron Goddess of Mercy, we found ourselves deep in the mountains of the Fujian province. We were seated at a table, being served tea by a grower who spoke only the local dialect, which meant the two of us could communicate only through expression and gesture.

This woman poured hot water from the teapot into a little bowl with tea leaves in it and set the bowl down in front of me. I reached out to pick it up, only to have her swat my hand out of the way, reach for the bowl, and dump the water out. Confused, I watched as, once again, she poured water from the teapot with the same strained tea leaves into the bowl. Again, I reached for it, and again, she pushed my hand out of the way, smiling as she did so.

This same series of events repeated itself a third time, but this time, I didn't reach for the bowl.

The fourth time, the woman poured tea from the teapot into the bowl, then gestured for me to drink it. Tentatively, I did. It was magical—full, floral, crisp, and light.

This was my introduction to the gong fu ritual of tea preparation. Although the ritual was simple enough, this woman was taking the time to awaken the leaf through multiple steepings to allow it to open and expand so that the natural oils of the tea could become entrenched in the liquid. She was taking her time and slowing things down so that I could immerse myself more fully in a sensory experience.

Of course, teatime in America doesn't usually look like this. But that doesn't mean tea isn't still rife for ritualistic use. In my mind at least, it's precisely all the trappings of modern daily life that make ritual more important today than ever before. Of all the benefits tea offers, the biggest benefit I see to tea is that it promotes ritual. I believe that now more than ever, we need these acts of ritual built into specific times of our day to create motivation and peace. It's from this place that we can find inspiration.

People often think of Americans as selfish. That stereotype always puzzles me because I think of Americans as the opposite. I think we tend to be quite selfless in that we're almost always willing to do way more for others and for our professional endeavors than we are for ourselves. But this isn't necessarily healthy or positive. Sometimes it can result in jealousy or in the desire to compare our own lives with what we see on social media. This can lead down a path of self-doubt and even self-destruction. Therein lies the great value and extreme health benefit of tea: preparing and drinking tea offers us the opportunity to narrow in on ourselves, on the moment, and on the experience at hand. Ironically, taking these moments to slow down wakes up a tremendous amount of additional time in the day.

The act of preparing, serving, and drinking tea is a ritual, even though many may not identify it as such. It's a ritual that extends beyond generations, politics, and time. Tea offers the opportunity to dedicate a slice of time in your day to being present and mindful. There is the opportunity to focus on the process of, first, making the tea as you boil the water and prepare the tea bag. And then there is the ritual of sipping and enjoying it, homing in on the senses it awakens. Put together, the entire experience provides us with permission and reason to stop and just *be* for a moment.

There are also biological reasons why it's important to drink tea in a ritualistic way to fully absorb its impact. From an Ayurvedic perspective, you actually begin to digest tea even as it's being steeped. Before you ever take a sip of your tea, your body is drinking it in through its other senses. While the tea is being brewed, your body kicks off a predigestive process that's triggered through the mere smell and sight of the herbs and botanicals. This is followed by another predigestive experience as you taste the tea. From there, the process continues as the herbs and botanicals are absorbed into your body while you actively digest the tea. The postdigestive effect then kicks in, which happens on a deeper subcellular level as your tissues, blood cells, and bones absorb the tea. Believe it or not, that final stage of postdigestion can last for a full twenty-one days. Of course, I'm not suggesting you stay in ritual for three full weeks, but I *am* suggesting that it's important to remain in a mindful, intentional state—in other words, a state of ritual—as all of this begins to take effect while you make and drink the tea.

I view tea as providing three primary experiences: blooming, expanding, and connecting. If you're quiet and still enough to notice what's happening as you drink tea, you might notice that a certain opening happens as you drink it, as if you are blossoming from within. From this blossoming, an expansion occurs. You expand to a higher level of thinking, your emotions relax, and anxiety is reduced. I'm not the only person who thinks this either. Poetry dating back thousands of years expresses this same sentiment.

In addition to all of this, any tea lover will tell you that tea elevates the moment. Tea connects us. In so many cultures, it's a natural element of hospitality. There's a particularly special energy to sipping on a cup of tea with another person. It slows everything down and brings you together in a shared sensory experience.

Aside from that human-to-human connection, rituals also allow us the opportunity to attain a higher level of development in our minds through which we can connect with and strengthen our connection to those things beyond ourselves. Some might call it the universe, but I personally choose not to label it. I just know there's a universal connectivity available to us. I've experienced it, and so have many other people I know. Of course, there are many ways to get there, but a lot of them tend to be ritualistic in nature. My ritual just happens to be tea. Preparing and drinking tea is one of the things that allows me to slow down and be present in a way that's necessary to connect.

I believe that ritual creates a sense of purpose. In this world that's often so out of our control, rituals are as close as we get to achieving a sense of it. Through those moments of ritual and the purpose that results, we can take ownership of our lives and how we view and interact with the world. Ritual offers a pause point, during which we can get quiet, get into the moment, regroup, and reset.

ENJOYING TEA AS RITUAL

In Matthew Kelly's bestselling book *The Rhythm of Life*, he writes: "On the one hand, we all want to be happy. On the other hand, we all know the things that make us happy, but we don't do those things. Why? Simple. We are too busy. Too busy doing what? Too busy trying to be happy." This is the tea paradox. We often feel like we don't have time to make tea, but making tea *gives* us time. That process and its impact create a deep, long-lasting level of happiness.

In the modern world, we're at a point where we have to seek out moments to go analog—tea offers a prime opportunity.

Certain ritualistic practices require a lot of preparation, time, and supplies. Tea does not. All it really takes to drink tea in a ritualistic way is the willingness to slow yourself down and observe yourself in the moment in which you are preparing, serving, and drinking your tea. Allow yourself the space to *be* there in that moment. If you do this, the process can be almost spiritual. It's really about a mindset.

Making tea draws upon all of our senses. It keeps us present. We are swept up in the aroma of boiling leaves as the tea is prepared. We can breathe in the warmth of a fire, stovetop, or other heat source as the pot warms up. We feel the weight of the pot as we begin to pour the tea into a cup. Our eyes drink the richness of watching the fluid rush to fill a cup. In that moment, we are restored. Calmed not just be the tea itself but by the ritualistic motions of making it.

Be intentional as you prepare and drink your tea. Give yourself the time to be present for it. Turn off that podcast you're listening to, stop scrolling through your newsfeed, and allow yourself the opportunity to really *be* there, even as you boil your water and prepare your tea.

Notice how this simple process of preparation opens up a few moments for mindfulness as you boil the water, select the leaves, and prepare your pot or cup. Notice how hands-on you are as you go about this timeless and ritualistic, sensory and connective process. I've mentioned how intentional we are at Art of Tea about the energy we infuse into the product, and it's equally true that your energy seeps into the tea along with the herbs. In this process, you have the opportunity to infuse love, intention, and energy into each cup of tea you offer to yourself and to others. Take the moments when you're steeping your tea to simply be in silence and to absorb the moment.

Find a calm, quiet place to enjoy your tea. Breathe in and notice the smells. As you sip, make a point of letting the tea pass over each part of your tongue so that you can be present for each different flavor. Different sections of the tongue sense different tastes, so you want to expose as much of your tongue as possible to the tea. The tip of your tongue detects sweetness. Can you notice that sweet first experience as you sip? In the middle of your tongue, you will experience sour, salty, and spicy tastes. And at the back of your tongue, you pick up on bitter and astringent flavors. Notice how much can happen in just a few seconds' time.

After you finish your tea, notice how your state has shifted. Notice how giving yourself that time and those moments has impacted your state of mind for the better.

Slow down, connect with yourself, and enjoy.

CHAPTER SEVEN

BECOME A TEA EXPERT

People often tell me they're intimidated by tea or afraid that they're going to somehow mess it up. I always remind them that it's just leaves and water. An enjoyable cup of tea really comes down to starting with great tea from a solid supplier. Supermarket tea is generally of a lower quality to begin with. This is compounded by the fact that it's often left sitting in a warehouse or on a shelf. This impacts taste because flavor is impacted by the conditions tea is kept in and the amount of time that passes before consumption.

Outside of that, in this chapter, we're going to cover the things that will help guarantee the best cup of tea possible, including some information about different types of tea, brewing tips, and other information to help you extract the best flavor from your tea.

WHAT IS TEA?

Let's start with the most basic question of all: What is tea? This question begs answering because we actually call many things tea in the vernacular that are not technically so. In the strictest sense, tea must include leaves from a plant called *Camellia sinensis*. There are three major varietals of *Camellia sinensis* and thousands of subvarieties. The specific type of tea is determined by how much those leaves are oxidized, which refers to the amount of oxygen they're exposed to upon picking, and the heating elements used on the leaves, such as coal or wood. Tea type is also impacted by how the leaves are massaged, baked, steamed, or dried. If the leaves aren't dried quickly, they'll wilt soon after being plucked from the stem. As the chlorophyll in the leaf begins to break down, the leaf darkens, and tannins are released. It's actually pretty incredible that the potential of a tea leaf—and whether it goes on to qualify as a black, green, white tea type or anything else—is unleashed based on the leaf's exposure to air.

All of this might lead you to believe that there are only a limited selection of "real teas" in the world, but that's not true at all. In fact, there are virtually unlimited nuances of variation possible amongst teas. These variations are dependent upon a number of factors between when the leaf is plucked and blended, including not only how it's processed but also which florals, fruits, spices, and other elements are added to the mixture. Not to mention the fact that leaves are impacted by natural cycles such as season and rainfall, which determine the lightness, depth, and flavor of the tea.

Now, what's *not* tea? If it's not from *Camellia sinensis*, then it's not tea. There are plenty of beverages out there that contain herbal blends and fruit infusions and are labeled as tea but are more accurately tisanes. Tisanes are a caffeine-free blend that consists of herbs, botanicals, and fruits and that are prepared like tea. For example, chamomile isn't a tea; it's a super yummy tisane. It's great, but it's not tea. Tisanes are also delicious and can serve many of the same purposes and benefits of tea. In fact, we make several blends of tisanes at Art of Tea. But for as much as the phrase "herbal tea" is used today, it's actually an oxymoron. Your drink is either one or the other: herbal or tea.

Tea and Caffeine

Here's a fun fact for you: tea leaves actually have a higher caffeine content than coffee. *However,* there's a "but" here. Although dry tea leaves have more caffeine by weight than coffee, your actual cup of tea doesn't contain more caffeine than your cup of coffee. The reason for this is that more dried coffee is used per cup than dry tea per cup, so a cup of steeped tea contains significantly less caffeine than a similarly sized cup of coffee.

Most studies show that tea contains between 40 and 120 mg of caffeine per 8-ounce serving. To put this in perspective, coffee has about 80 to 206 mg of caffeine per 8-ounce serving.

Caffeine levels in tea are directly related to how long the tea is steeped. The longer it's steeped, the higher the amount of caffeine it contains.

TEA TYPES

Tea offers such a great opportunity for discovery. And trying out different types of tea is a great opportunity to practice mindfulness as you immerse yourself into the sensory experience. As you drink, notice how the different varieties smell and taste. How do they make you feel as you drink them? How about *after* you drink them? Are they calming or enlivening? And how do they impact you as you move forward throughout your day and night?

When I was studying Ayurveda, I used to fast each Thursday, digesting only one tea or herb as a beverage for the entire day.

I did this because I wanted to really understand—in a practical way—the taste and effect the tea or botanical had on my mind and body. I'm not necessarily recommending this method, but it does help develop a deeper understanding of how your body reacts to a particular type of tea or herb.

To get you started down the right path, following is some information about each major tea type, including where it comes from, how to prepare it, how it tastes, and the benefits it offers. Each section will also include a listing of some specific variants for each type of tea, but know that there are a *ton* of variants of each type of tea. These listings are just a starting place to help you gain an understanding of some of the most noteworthy, popular, and delicious variants for each category of tea.

BLACK TEA

What much of the world calls black tea is alternately known as red tea in China because of its rich, reddish infusion—and also because China already calls pu-erh (see Chapter Four) dark tea. Whatever you call it, though, black tea is the most popular tea on the planet.

China and India are the two major producers of black tea globally. However, India consumes more than 70 percent of the tea it makes, which means high-quality black tea from India can be hard to come by.

Black tea is so popular and in demand because it delivers such a robust flavor. Its rich flavor and black appearance are a result of the fact that this tea is 100 percent cooked and oxidized. This methodology mimics the process that used to happen naturally when tea was transported from origin to destination by camelback over a long period of time with nightly stops around the campfire.

Much like people with a refined palate can home in on wine by origin, the same holds true when it comes to black tea. These unique flavor characteristics are the result of factors like soil, elevation, and heating elements. Black teas also offer a lot of room to play when it comes to blending because it's possible to play up their nuances in particularly creative ways.

Drink Black Tea Like an Expert

Amount of tea: 1 teaspoon per 8-ounce cup
Water temperature: 206° F
Steep time: 3-5 minutes*
Resteeping: Black tea can be resteeped three to five times; the flavor will decrease with each steeping.

*The longer a cup of black tea is steeped, the higher its caffeine content will be. The caffeine content will decrease with each resteeping.

While oxidization does lower the levels of naturally existing caffeine in black teas, it still has a high caffeine content as compared to other teas and about half the amount of caffeine found in a cup of coffee. The caffeine content is slightly higher in Indian black teas than those of Chinese origin due to the different strains of leaves used. Black tea also includes L-theanine, which provides a mindful boost minus the midday crash. This dark, richly flavored tea is great to drink upon waking to get you up and going and focused for the day ahead.

Today, black tea accounts for more than 90 percent of the tea sold in the US, most of which is enjoyed as iced tea.

Black Tea Variants

Assam (India)—With a bold and malty flavor, Assam rivals the potent punch of coffee. It's a great base for blending and holds up well against multiple steepings.

Ceylon (Sri Lanka)—The experience of this tea is dependent upon where it's harvested. Some Ceylon is a light, golden color with a round, feathery finish, while others offer a deep, mahogany tincture and bolder taste. Ceylon is considered one of the finest teas in the world.

Congu (China)—Slightly sweet in flavor, congu is brisk and rich. It is often used as a starter element in kombucha tea.

Darjeeling (India)—Like champagne is to Champagne, France, the only true Darjeeling comes from Darjeeling, India. Some experts believe Darjeeling is more of an oolong tea than a black tea because of the Taiwanese equipment and techniques used to produce it. It has a smooth, bright flavor with muscatel overtones and a slightly floral finish. It leaves behind a subtle hint of lingering astringency on the palate. Many argue Darjeeling is one of the best black teas in the world.

(continued on page 128)

Keemun mao feng (China)—This tea is historically revered and has been passed down from generation to generation. Keemun mao feng is prized for its aromatic properties. It's vibrant and contains notes of pine, cocoa, and marshmallow.

Lapsang souchong (China)—One of the first black teas introduced to the West, lapsang souchong is known for its smoky flavor. Historically, that flavor was absorbed from the campfires of traveling caravans, but today it's recreated by smoking the leaves over pine needles. This tea pairs great with savory dishes.

GREEN TEA

Drink Green Tea Like an Expert

Amount of tea: 1 teaspoon per 8-ounce cup

Water temperature: 140°-165° (Japanese green teas); 175°-185° (Chinese green teas)

Steep time: 1-2 minutes (Japanese green teas); 3-5 minutes (Chinese green teas)*

Resteeping: 2-3 times before flavor degradation occurs

The longer a cup of green tea is steeped, the higher the caffeine content will be. The caffeine content will decrease with each resteeping.

Green tea has been consumed for longer than any other type of tea. It continues to be one of the most popular types of tea in the world to this day, in large part thanks to its superfood properties.

China and Japan are the two primary sources of green tea. While both of their teas are made of the same leaves and prepared in similar ways, the final result can taste quite different. Think about it like this: imagine you go to a farmer's market and buy two bundles of asparagus. You wok-fire one of the batches and steam the other. The wok-fired asparagus is charred on the outside while sweet and dense on the inside. The steamed bundle is greener, maintains more of its natural flavor, and has more of a fresh crispness to it. Either way, you have asparagus—it's just that the preparation technique and ultimate taste are different.

The difference between Chinese and Japanese green teas is very similar to this.

If you eat Chinese and Japanese foods, you know that the cuisines have different flavor profiles. Chinese food tends to be wok-fired, crispy, and hot, while Japanese cuisine tends toward rice, steamed vegetables, and seafood, often flavored with salt. The green teas from each of these regions match their food profiles. Green tea from China is smoky and grassy, while green tea from Japan errs toward fresh, bright, flavors—the epitome of umami.

Over its thousands of years of existence, the process of producing green tea hasn't changed much. It continues to be hand-harvested and shaped, often with the help of simple, age-old machinery that has been passed down from one generation to the next. The leaves are plucked when slightly withered and immediately cooked to preserve their green quality and to prevent oxidation. Because of this, green teas have a higher concentration of chlorophyll, polyphenols, and antioxidants than other types of tea. Green teas are largely differentiated from one another by the way in which the leaves are heated, which varies greatly from one region to the next. The two primary heating methods are pan-firing (China) and steaming (Japan). As a result of these different processes, pan-fired green tea is often pale green in color, while steamed green tea is bright green.

Green tea is popular for its well-earned reputation as a superfood, which offers a number of benefits, including its potential to help combat and prevent cancer, reduce heart disease, increase metabolism, and calm the nervous system. (For even more about these benefits, see the "Matcha Tea" section that follows.) Green tea is also a great "booster" tea to drink when you're feeling uninspired or want a burst of motivation.

Green Tea Variants

Genmaicha (Japan)–Popularly known as popcorn tea, genmaicha is made with green tea and roasted brown rice. Lore has it that farmers used to add rice to stretch out their tea supplies by adding rice, which is why this is also known as the people's tea. It has a slightly roasted hue and a crisp yet roasted finish.

(continued on page 131)

Gunpowder (China)—This name reflects the process through which the tea is made; the leaves are hand-shaped into small spheres that resemble gunpowder. It has a slightly brisk, smoky flavor and serves as the primary ingredient in Moroccan mint tea because the gunpowder rounds out and balances the sharpness of the mint.

Gyokuro / Jade Dew (Japan)—With its sweet, grassy finish, this variant is considered the most precious and highly sought-after green tea. Gyokuro is shade-grown for up to two weeks to bring up the leaf's rich chlorophyll, resulting in the tea's signature bright-green hue.

Hojicha (Japan)—Unlike most Japanese teas, hojicha leaves are roasted over charcoal rather than steamed. This impacts the color of the leaves, and the tea is reddish-brown with hints of caramel and a slightly toasted finish.

Kukicha (Japan)—Also known as twig tea, kukicha is comprised of twigs, stems, and stalks. It's slightly roasted and a bit more oxidized than most green teas, which gives it a nutty taste and a round, thick flavor.

Longjing/Dragonwell (China)—Flat, sword-shaped leaves are panfried to create this varietal, which has a vibrant jade-green hue and a fresh, clean, mellow flavor and aroma.

Sencha (Japan)—The most common green tea in Japan, sencha has an astringent taste with bright grassy afternotes.

Yun Wu / Cloudmist (China)—Aptly named, this tea is harvested at a much higher altitude, smothered in clouds. It has a light, salty, sweet taste.

MATCHA

Drink Matcha Like an Expert

Amount of tea: 1 teaspoon per 6- to 8-ounce cup

Water temperature: 160° to keep the grassy texture and color intact

Preparation: Because matcha is ground, it's not steeped like other types of tea. To make matcha, preheat a tea bowl with a small amount of boiling water and moisten a tea whisk. Scoop in the matcha, and add the remaining water to fill the bowl. Hold the bowl firmly with one hand while using the other hand to whisk from left to right to form frothy bubbles. As you whisk, break up any small lumps of matcha with the tip of your whisk to ensure optimal flavor and a smooth, creamy texture. Finally, hold the whisk in the middle of your foam and allow the liquid inside of the whisk to draw off.

Translated, *matcha* means "stone-ground green tea." The difference between matcha and regular gyokuro green tea is that the stems are removed from the leaves, and the leaves are then ground into a very fine powder.

The art of producing, preparing, and consuming matcha began as a ritual performed by Zen Buddhist monks in China. They believed matcha brought them clarity, mental focus, and calm, and thus used it as a part of their meditation practice.

Matcha was introduced to Japan when a Zen monk named Eisai traveled from China to Japan. Japanese Zen monasteries then adopted it as an important part of their rituals. As we've discussed, matcha was also prominent amongst Samurai warriors—who sensed the same benefits the monks did—and used it as a way of improving their energy and focus during battle.

Over time, the popularity of matcha decreased in China while simultaneously increasing in Japan. Since matcha was difficult to produce, it wasn't until the *uji* production method was created in 1738 that it became available for wider adoption in Japan. The Japanese continued to change and perfect their own unique process for creating matcha, which is why it's commonly more associated with their culture today, even though it originated from China. Matcha made its way into the Western culture as a healthy alternative to espresso and a delicious, nutrient-dense addition to smoothies and lattes.

The process of preparing matcha to drink is steeped in ritual. Historically, it was brewed and presented in a performance-based tea ceremony called *chanoyu*, which rests on the four core principles of harmony, respect, purity, and tranquility. The process might look simple, but it's actually incredibly precise and detailed. In fact, it takes nearly ten years for a master to perfect the *chanoyu* ceremony.

While all variants of green tea are classified as superfoods, matcha is particularly known for its health benefits. Since matcha is made with the entire leaf and then ground into powder and mixed into water, it retains all of its nutrients in a way that steeping green tea does not. Green tea loses some of its nutrients in the process of steeping and then discarding the leaves rather than consuming them. So, while matcha and green tea both include the same properties, those properties are much more present and pronounced in matcha.

In each delicious sip of matcha, you are drinking in:

- **Antioxidants**—Catechins are powerful antioxidants that may increase metabolism, endurance, and reduce free radicals and toxins, making those who consume matcha less susceptible to illness.

- **Tannins**—Also known as polyphenols, tannins are micronutrients that come from plants and are found in teas and wines.

- **Amino acids**—L-theanine is an amino acid that offers the energy boost of caffeine minus the crash. It's said to improve learning, memory, and creativity.

As if all of this wasn't enough, matcha also includes a much higher amount of caffeine than green tea does, again because the entire leaf is consumed.

Research points to the fact that all of these properties can help prevent and alleviate cancer, reduce the risk of heart disease, promote weight loss, increase exercise endurance, enhance cognition, improve oral and dental health, and relieve stress and arthritis. Matcha's fine powder form delivers a concentrated amount of antioxidants, which can help the human body neutralize the free radicals caused by the stress and toxicity of everyday life. It helps support metabolism and is rich in absorbable fiber. Not only that, but this fresh, aromatic tea will help you feel more awake at any time of the day when you need a little boost, and its full-bodied flavor and slightly sweet aftertaste are a wonderful way to experience true umami.

Matcha Classifications

There are many grades of matcha, but following are the two main classifications. When selecting your matcha, you want to look for vibrancy and a fresh, full mouthfeel without a lot of astringency to the finish.

Ceremonial grade—This matcha is made with top-quality Japanese green tea, the leaves of which are ground between two large stones until they become powder. It's a noisy, tedious process that produces only about thirty grams of matcha per hour. Ceremonial-grade matcha results in a vibrant, dark-green tea that appears almost emerald in color. The taste is less astringent and more complex than grade A matcha. Ceremonial-grade matcha is best used when preparing hot or iced matcha tea.

Grade A—Sometimes called cooking-grade matcha, grade A is of lower quality than ceremonial-grade matcha but excellent for use in recipes for smoothies and baked goods. It's also a fantastic base for matcha drinks, like hot or iced lattes.

OOLONG TEA

Drink Oolong Tea Like an Expert

Amount of tea: 1 teaspoon per 8-ounce cup (rolled oolong) / 1 tablespoon per 8-ounce cup (longleaf oolong)
Water temperature: 185°–206°
Steep time: 3–5 minutes*
Resteeping: Multiple times; the taste will improve and transform with each resteeping, with the fourth or fifth steeping generally being the best.

The longer a cup of oolong tea is steeped, the higher the caffeine content will be. The caffeine content will decrease by about one-third with each resteeping.

Translated from its Chinese origin, the word *oolong* means "black dragon." This makes sense because in their novel state, these leaves actually look like little black dragons.

Oolongs are known as a connoisseur's tea because so much craft and delicacy goes into creating them. Generally speaking, oolongs come from China or Taiwan, although some interesting styles are beginning to come out of Nepal and Sri Lanka. Harvesting and crafting oolongs is often considered to be a family affair, entrenched in unique traditions, processes, and secrets. Throughout the villages where oolongs are produced, families are often known for making certain styles of oolong tea. It's a lot like if you went to a town in Italy and asked which family made the best spaghetti sauce—everyone uses the same ingredients, but the different decisions each family makes along the way impact the ultimate flavor of the sauce.

Harvesting and baking the leaves can be an all-day process. The leaves are often picked in the morning as the fog rolls off. They're then withered and semioxidized in the sun, anywhere from 1 to 99 percent. This means that oolongs can smell and taste like a green tea (less oxidized), a black tea (more oxidized), or somewhere in between. You can think about it like an apple. If you bite into an apple, then set it down for one hour, it will oxidize less than it does if you were to bite into it, then set the apple down for twelve hours. The effects of oxidization in the case of oolong tea are also impacted by factors such as altitude, humidity, and time of year.

After being shade-dried, the leaves are tossed in a bamboo basket. As the leaves crash back down into the basket, they are crushed, which brings the juice inside of the leaf to the surface. They are rolled and massaged, and then the baking process begins when the right moment arrives. Baking is generally done once the humidity starts to lift, which means the process sometimes does not start until as late as midnight.

The specifics of this baking process often involve family secrets and ancient techniques. A family might use damp wood or dry wood; they could opt for charcoal or gas. All of these decisions impact the taste of the tea and result in a unique flavor. Finally, the leaves are curled or rolled into crispy shapes that resemble tiny black dragons.

Oolong Tea Types and Variants

Bao Zhong (Taiwan)—Because it's not as oxidized as other oolongs and has a brilliant jade-green appearance, bao zhong is close to a green tea. It has a slightly floral flavor with crisp overtones and a delicate finish.

Da Hong Pao / Big Red Robe (China)—This mountain-grown tea is considered one of the most prized oolong varietals. It packs a unique, woodsy flavor that transforms on the palate with each steep.

Ti Kuan Yin / Iron Goddess of Mercy (China)—One of the most revered oolongs, this varietal has a smooth, slightly floral flavor and aroma.

Wuyi oolong (China)—This tea is a perfect intro to the world of oolong with its heady, floral aroma and rich, round finish.

PU-ERH TEA

Drink Pu-erh Tea Like an Expert

Amount of tea: 1 tablespoon per 8-ounce cup
Water temperature: 206°
Steep time: Begin with a quick flush of hot water to open up the leaves and give them a quick rinse; then empty the water and refill with fresh hot water to steep for 5-7 minutes.
Resteeping: 10-12 times before flavor degradation occurs

The longer a cup of pu-erh tea is steeped, the higher the caffeine content will be. However, the amount of caffeine content to begin with depends on how old the pu-erh is—the younger the pu-erh, the higher the caffeine content.

One time, I was meeting with a wine sommelier at a hotel, and I poured him some pu-erh. He smelled it and said, "Wow, this is amazing." Then he took a sip and said, "Hmm. So interesting."

As he tasted the pu-erh, three other people stood around him watching. They leaned in to see what his final verdict was. What adjectives was he going to use to describe the taste of the tea?

The sommelier took another sip, put the cup down, and said thoughtfully, "It tastes like…manure."

Pu-erh is the tea equivalent of a really stinky cheese or funky wine; it's an experience. The taste of pu-erh is very smooth and round, but the aromatics are like your grandmother's attic or a forest floor. It has a bold taste that can vary based on the conditions and environmental factors in which it's grown. These flavors run the gamut from smooth and fruity to peaty and grassy to musky, herbal, and earthy.

In the Far East, pu-erh tea is known as black tea, but the rest of the world refers to it as pu-erh because it was first developed in the town of Pu-erh, located in the Yunnan province of China. To this day, pu-erh must originate from the mountains of this region to rightfully earn its name.

Pu-erh is harvested from a larger leaf strain of *Camellia sinensis* known as *dayeh*. The ancient trees that are home to these mature leaves are said to be between five hundred and one thousand years old. After the leaves are harvested, they're steamed and then cold-stored in a damp, dark cave or room for about ninety days. In the course of that time, bacteria attaches itself to the leaves, and that bacteria starts to slowly cook or ferment the leaves. That fermentation process is a distinguishing attribute of pu-erh. It causes the leaves to darken and change flavors, and allows the tea to improve with age like a fine wine, retaining its freshness for as long as fifty years.

After the initial cold-storage period, pu-erh is then stored in a dry room, either in a loose or brick format. At this point, three types of pu-erh might emerge: raw (aged for a year), half-baked (aged for five years), or full-baked (aged for seven to ten years).

Pu-erh was initially transported by large caravans of mules and horses along established routes that were known as Tea Horse Roads. Traders bartered for the tea in the markets of Pu-erh and then took them home to sell. It's because of this long journey that producers started to ferment the pu-erh tea leaves—it served the practical purpose of keeping the tea fresh.

Drinkers soon realized that pu-erh helped with digestion, a direct side effect of the fermentation. Because it was affordable, pu-erh became a popular household tea. Over time, it became more and more prized and served as a powerful tool for bartering amongst traveling merchants.

Although pu-erh is only now being introduced to mainstream tea drinkers in the Western world, it's considered very valuable globally. Pay attention, and you'll notice that these days, pu-erh is being more and more frequently touted in the media for its health benefits.

How to Drink Pu-erh

Pu-reh is most often prepared in a Yixing teapot or gaiwan tea bowl. It is often served gong fu style, which means that you will want to steep it three times before serving to bring out the maximum flavor. To do this, immerse the leaves in hot water for a few seconds to flush and awaken the leaves before pouring your first tasting round and steeping them again. They can be steeped for as many as ten to twelve times before beginning to lose their flavor.

Pu-erh is best enjoyed when slurped. This exposes the tea to air, which activates the pur-reh's diverse flavors and provides greater contact with your taste buds.

WHITE TEA

Drink White Tea Like an Expert

Amount of tea: 1 teaspoon per 8-ounce cup
Water temperature: 175°–185°
Steep time: 1–3 minutes
Resteeping: Generally not recommended, as the flavor of white tea quickly diminishes.

Of all the tea types, white tea has the most delicate flavor profile. For this reason, it's not one of the more sought-after teas in Asia. In North America, however, many people enjoy white tea for its health benefits. Research from the Linus Pauling Institute points to its effects on fighting cancer and heart disease, as well as helping to increase collagen.

White tea arrives in your cup in a needle shape, sometimes with buds attached. It consists of the new, young tea leaves and buds, and is only harvested for a few weeks each spring in the northern district of Fujian, China (in fact, only tea that comes from Fujian can technically be called white tea). Not only does the harvesting season last for just a few weeks, but the leaves can also only be picked on days when it's not rainy or humid.

Harvesting and preparing white tea is a very minimalistic process, which leads many people to think of it as a raw tea that offers even more beneficial properties than green and black teas. To harvest, growers pick just the top of the bushes before the leaves fully open. These leaves have to be picked quickly to halt the oxidation process and capture only the best first flush of leaves and buds. It's such a delicate process that, many centuries ago, the task was entrusted only to virgins wearing white gloves.

After the leaves are picked, they're put out to dry, often in baskets, and then put through a warm air-dryer type of process (in the case of silver needle) or scattered across heat vents (in the case of white peony), depending upon the varietal of white tea. This is a very delicate process, and great care is taken to avoid cooking the leaves or causing any sort of fermentation process to begin.

As white tea steeps, the fuzz falls off of the leaf (especially with the silver needle varietal of white tea), which can create a shimmering effect. In fact, Art of Tea works with some high-end spas that forgo champagne and, instead, serve cold-brewed white tea to their clients in flutes. Served like this, white tea offers that same luxurious sort of experience as champagne, along with a host of health benefits.

White Tea Types and Variants

Silver Needle—This is the highest-quality and most sought-after white tea. It has a pale golden flush with a sweet, floral aroma and a light, woodsy body.

Shou Mei—This taste is darker and fuller than other white teas, with a bold finish.

White Peony—A premium quality tea, white peony has a sweet yet nutty taste with a slightly roasted finish.

PREPARE YOUR TEA LIKE A PRO

Like I promised at the beginning of this chapter, making tea isn't complicated. But there *are* a few simple best practices, some of which apply to all teas and others of which apply to specific types. Following is everything you need to know to maximize the flavor and potential of your next cup of tea.

PRECISION MATTERS

Adding more tea leaves to your tea doesn't necessarily equate better flavor. This isn't something you'll need to worry about if you're using prepackaged tea bags; however, you *will* want to properly measure out your tea if you're using loose leaves.

As a general rule of thumb, you will want to use one level teaspoon of tea per serving for smaller-leaved teas, such as black tea, and a heaping teaspoon per serving for fluffier leaves, like white tea. If you are making multiple servings of tea at once in a teapot, add an additional teaspoon to the recommended amount of tea per serving. This extra scoop is for the teapot. In other words, if you have a four-cup teapot, put in five teaspoons of tea. The extra teaspoon will add a bit more body to the tea.

Refer to the chart at the end of this chapter for a quick reference guide for the proper amount of tea to steep per every six to eight ounces of water. If you realize over time that you happen to prefer your tea stronger, simply add a bit more tea for the same recommended steep time.

CHOOSE YOUR WATER WISELY

Steeped tea is composed of 98 percent water. This means that if your water isn't of a high quality, your tea won't be either. Whenever possible, use clean, freshly drawn water sources or filtration systems to preserve the flavor of your tea.

KNOW YOUR TEMPERATURE

Different types of tea require different temperatures of boiled water to unlock their optimal flavor. The less processed the tea is, the lower the temperature should be. As tea is processed and aged, its profile becomes more distinct and heartier. This means the tea has a greater ability to maintain its integrity when steeped in boiling water.

Along the tea spectrum, black tea is the most processed type of tea and requires the hottest temperature water. White tea is the least processed and, thus, requires the lowest temperature water. Delicate tea leaves, such as white tea, will wilt too quickly under the intensity of boiled water and begin to taste bitter. Worse than that, the leaves will become damaged, which compromises their health and relaxation properties. For specific tea type temperatures, please see the chart at the end of this chapter.

The easiest way to determine the temperature of your water is with a basic kitchen thermometer. If your boiled water is hotter than the temperature indicated on the chart that follows, you can simply let it be for a few minutes until the water cools to the appropriate temperature. If you follow the same routine and use the same tea on a regular basis, you can simply notice how long it generally takes the water to cool to the appropriate temperature and build that waiting time into your ritual. Another alternative is to use ice cubes to cool the water—in fact, we recommend that the restaurants we work with use this tactic. Add an ice cube to your mug or pot before pouring in the boiling water so that the coolness is evenly distributed. From there, you can add one ice cube at a time as necessary to lower the temperature. Again, you can use a kitchen thermometer the first few times to notice how many cubes it takes you to get to your desired temperature, then build a routine around that.

Finally, I strongly recommend that you refrain from microwaving tea water. Yes, microwaves are efficient, but in addition to taking away from the mindfulness of using boiled water, microwaved water decreases the quality of your cup of tea. Microwaves will lower the accuracy of the heated water, and they also don't heat water evenly. To avoid cool spots, you'll have to overheat your water, which can destroy the aromatic compounds in tea and create a bitter flavor.

This applies to reheating as well. Rather than reheating cooled tea in a microwave, instead, invest in a covered container (such as a mug or tumbler) that will keep your tea warmer over a longer period of time.

Teapot 101

People often don't realize how many options there are for teapots until they go to pick one out and are quickly overwhelmed. Here are some basics to guide you along the right path.

CAST IRON

Cast-iron teapots are a good choice for all types of tea since they infuse easily. Also, because they were originally designed to hold hot water, cast iron pots are excellent for retaining heat over a long period of time. The only drawback is that they can develop rust around their rim over time. That can be cleaned by rubbing a used tea leaf along the rusted area because the tannins halt the oxidization of the iron.

CERAMIC

Ceramic teapots work equally well for all types of tea. They're sturdy and easy to clean and don't impact the flavor of the tea since their inside is glazed or coated. They also retain heat well and will keep tea warm over a longer period of time. The only downsides to ceramics are that they can break and stain.

GLASS

Glass teapots are great if you like to drink blooming teas because you can actually see the leaves unravel and the flowers blossom, which is a very meditative process, much like watching a dance. This will help you determine when it's time to stop steeping. The glass also helps retain the heat evenly throughout the pot. The downside to glass teapots is that they can be prone to breakage since they're delicate (handwashing is recommended!), and the spout may stain.

(continued on page 148)

YIXING

If you prefer oolong or pu-erh teas, Yixing teapots are your best bet. Because the inside of this teapot is unglazed, it will collect minerals and oils over time, which will influence the flavors of the tea. Over time, you can steep your tea for shorter amounts of time because the flavors are already absorbed inside of the teapot. Eventually, you can just fill up the pot with hot water (no tea required) and end up with a delicious cup of tea. Because this pot reserves the flavor so well, it also means that the teapot must be reserved for only one type of tea. One trade-off is that the heat retention is not great for this type of pot.

CHOOSE YOUR INFUSER

If you're brewing loose-leaf tea rather than tea bags, you'll need to utilize an infuser to hold your tea leaves together so that they can be easily removed from the water once you finish steeping. Know your options as well as some of their pros and cons.

Single-Serve Reusable Infusers

This stand-alone accessory is small and generally made from metal, mesh, or silicon.

Single-serve infusers are economically and environmentally friendly since they can be used time and time again. However, they can be difficult to clean and offer limited space if you want to make more than one cup of tea at a time.

Mugs, Tumblers, and Teapots with Built-In Infusers

Mugs and tumblers with built-in infusers are great for on-the-go convenience. They do limit you to one serving of tea at a time, however.

Teapots with infusers resolve the multiple-cup-of-tea issue. Generally, these teapots can make about three cups of tea at a time. All of these options are environmentally and economically friendly.

Filter Bags

Filter bags are flexible in that they can be used for a single serving of tea and are also large enough to make multiple cups at a time when used in a teapot. Since they're disposable, filter bags don't require any cleaning, which is a huge win!

Of course, filter bags can be wasteful, depending upon the composition of the bag. Be intentional about selecting biodegradable filter bags, which are typically A-okay for the environment, and can even be tossed into your compost bin or buried in the garden like compost after use.

What about Iced Tea?

When it comes to the difference between hot and cold tea, you can think about it like pizza. When you eat a fresh, hot pizza, you pick up on the spicy, sour, and sharp notes. The next day, when you dive into the leftover cold slices, you're eating the same ingredients, but the more round and sweet notes come to the surface. The same goes for tea.

(continued on page 150)

The exact same tea might taste different, depending upon whether you drink it hot or cold. For iced teas, my go-to picks are classic black teas, green tea, pomegranate, or peach teas because they brew so nicely in this format.

To brew a single cup of iced tea, all you have to do is brew your tea as you normally would and place your mug in the refrigerator for a few minutes. To finish, add ice to a glass, pour the cooled tea over it, and enjoy. Simple, right?

To make a larger batch of iced tea, you have two primary options: cold brew and hot brew.

To cold-brew iced tea:

- Steep one 2-quart sachet or 7 teaspoons of loose-leaf tea (placed in a filter bag) in water heated to 160° or higher for 30 seconds.

- Keep the sachet in the pitcher

- Fill the pitcher with 8 cups of freshly drawn water.

- Cover and place the pitcher in your fridge for 8 to 10 hours.

- Remove the sachet or loose-leaf tea and enjoy!

- To hot-brew iced tea:

- Add one 2-quart sachet or 7 teaspoons of loose-leaf tea to a pitcher.

- Fill the pitcher with 3 cups of hot water.

(continued on page 151)

- Cover the pitcher and allow the tea to steep for 4 minutes.

- Remove the sachet or loose-leaf tea from the pitcher.

- Fill the pitcher with 5 cups of room-temperature water. (Cold will shock the tea and may cause the brew to become cloudy.)

- Stir and enjoy!

PUT DOWN THE MILK AND SUGAR

As a blender, I'm obviously a big proponent of drinking tea as is because taste profiles are so important to me. But, taste aside, there's a far more compelling reason to put down some of the additives people most frequently use.

Great quality tea should never require agave, sugar, milk, or cream. All of these additives change the dynamic of the tea and result in a less-than-optimal experience. The antioxidants found in tea bind to milk and sugar molecules. This means that adding milk or sugar in may reduce or negate the health benefits of your tea. If your cup of tea tastes like it needs any of these extras, something isn't quite right. Double-check your water temperature and brewing time. Also, sample different types of tea to discover which taste works best for your palate au naturel. Tea is always best enjoyed in its natural state to showcase its taste and distinct profiles, as well as to maximize its health properties.

Now, having said that, if you want to enhance the flavor of your tea, you can try some extras that mix well with the tea and bring in even *more* health benefits. Some of my favorites include mint, ginger slices, cardamom pods, cinnamon sticks, vanilla sticks, and licorice root. To include any of these, simply brew them along with your tea.

STORAGE MATTERS

High-quality tea doesn't spoil, but, as with most consumable products, the sooner it's enjoyed, the fresher and more potent it will be (with a few exceptions, such as pu-erh). You can preserve the flavor and freshness of your unflavored tea for up to eighteen months by properly storing it. Flavored teas (that is, teas with added aromatic compounds or natural oils) can last for up to twelve months.

Keep your tea in an airtight container and store that container away from heat, exposure to light, and moisture. Also, be aware that teas are fragile and can be easily altered by neighboring spices and aromas. Be sure to store your tea in an area where the leaves will not be permeated by other flavors or aromatics.

CommuniTea Tips
Tea Steeping Chart

TEA TYPE	WATER	6-8 OZ	TIME
White	175°-185°	1 tbsp	1-3 min
Green	180°-185°	1 tsp	3 min
Black	206°	1 tsp	3-5 min
Darjeeling	185°	1 tsp	3 min
Oolong Rolled	185°-206°	1 tsp	3-5 min
Oolong Long Leaf	185°-206°	1 tbsp	3-5 min
Tisane	206°	1 tbsp	5-7 min
Raw Pu-erh	195°	1 tbsp	3-5 min
*Half & Full Baked Pu-erh	206°	1 tbsp	3-5 min

Most teas may be steeped multiple times.
* First soak for 30 seconds, flush, then re-steep.

ARTOFTEA.COM

A FINAL NOTE TO READERS

Icontinue to be a work in process, but as I stand here in my mid-forties, there are a few things I can tell you for sure.

While I would never have chosen the tragedies of my early life, I can't change the fact that they happened. And because they did happen, I learned from them. I believe that people like me who suffer losses early in life are armed with the depth of wisdom that comes from moving forward despite pain and trauma. These people understand they have the ability to make it out of any circumstance. They develop within them a special brand of resilience and carry that forward into every situation, every single day.

Even in pain, there are gifts. I personally believe that's how it's meant to be. I believe that we human beings are a reflection of the universe, which is constantly creating and crashing into itself. Stars are colliding with other stars to create new stars, new formations, and new galaxies. We are meant to innovate, to create, to push, to build, and to celebrate the gorgeousness of this life in whatever way we feel most deeply called.

As I look back at that crossroads in my life when I could have become either a Rabbi or a tea master, I know that I followed the right path. I love learning, I love ancient texts, I love having a tribe, and I love ritual. While the rabbinical path certainly would have allowed me the opportunity to delve into all of those things, so does tea. The difference is that tea also opens up the playing field so that the impact I'm able to affect extends beyond religion, race, ethnicity, gender, and religion.

For as much as I'm happy with what I have accomplished so far both personally and professionally, I also know I'm not done yet. Based on my childhood, I adopted a survival mentality that has compelled me to constantly contemplate and reevaluate what success really means and whether or not I'm there yet. While I'm proud of what I've done, I also know that, for me, success won't really come until I've played a role in a mass movement of people being aware not just of my teas but of the impact *all* good tea has on people's lives. For me, that's what impact looks like.

As you know by now, I'm all about impact. One cup at a time.

TEA RECIPES

Tea is great for drinking on its own, and it also makes an excellent ingredient. At Art of Tea, we've designed and been inspired by a variety of recipes built around tea. We hope you have just as much fun playing with these recipes as we've had creating them.

I hope that you will share some of your favorite tea recipes with us, as well as stories of ritual and impact through tea at Facebook.com/theartoftea.

TEA DRINKS

CHAI LATTE

2 teaspoons Tali's Masala Chai (from Art of Tea)
6 ounces boiling water
1 cup whole milk
¼ cup brown sugar, packed
2 tablespoons French vanilla nondairy creamer
Whipped topping, optional
Ground nutmeg, optional

Steep the chai tea in the boiling water for 3–5 minutes, making sure to leave at least ¼ cup of the mug empty to reserve room for the latte mixture.

As the tea is steeping, combine the milk, brown sugar, and creamer into a small saucepan on medium heat. Heat the mixture until all of the ingredients are warm and the sugar is dissolved.

Pour the latte mixture into your tea mug. Top with a dollop of your desired whipped topping and sprinkle with ground nutmeg, if desired.

DALGONA MATCHA LATTE

1 egg white or 2 tablespoons of aquafaba (chickpea liquid)

1 tablespoon granulated sugar (white, turbinado, or cane)

½ teaspoon matcha or 1 Art of Tea Matchastick

1 cup milk or milk alternative

Whip the egg white until it's frothy and mostly stiff on a whisk, hand mixer, or handheld frother.

Add the sugar and continue whipping until stiff peaks form and the mixture sticks to the whisk.

Sift in the matcha and whisk until incorporated.

Add the milk to your desired drinking cup. Top it with the whipped matcha and enjoy!

ART OF ICED MATCHA MILK LATTE

½ teaspoon of matcha or 1 Art of Tea Matchastick

4 ounces cold water

4 ounces milk, frothed

Scoop the matcha into a bowl or wide cup, and add freshly drawn, cold, filtered water. Whisk the matcha with a handheld frother or matcha whisk until foam appears and the matcha is fully suspended in the water.

Pour the matcha into a glass half filled with ice. Use a handheld frother to froth your favorite milk, and add it on top of the matcha.

Dust the top of the drink with matcha to serve.

ART OF ICED MATCHA

½ teaspoon matcha or 1 Art of Tea Matchastick
1 cup cold water, divided into ½ cups
4 ice cubes

Add the matcha into a small bowl or wide cup. Add half of the cold water and whisk until foam appears and the matcha is fully suspended in the water. Add the remaining cold water and continue stirring until the matcha is fully mixed.

Place the ice cubes into a tall glass, pour in the matcha, and enjoy!

MINT MATCHA ICED TEA

2 cups cold filtered water, divided into 1-cup portions

½ teaspoon matcha or 1 Art of Tea Matchastick

4 ice cubes

1 lime, sliced

A few fresh mint leaves, to taste

Add the matcha into a small bowl or wide cup. Add half of the cold water and whisk until foam appears and the matcha is fully suspended in the water. Add the remaining cold water, ice, a squeeze of lime, and mint leaves to your liking. Continue stirring until the matcha is fully mixed.

Pour the drink into a tall glass, add additional ice if preferred, and garnish with mint leaves and a slice of lime.

TEA-TINIS AND MOCKTAILS

HIBISCUS COOLER SANGRIA

1 two-quart pouch Art of Tea Hibiscus Cooler (from Art of Tea)
4 cups boiling water
1 pound sliced fruit, such as apples, berries, or oranges

In a large container, brew the Hibiscus Cooler in the boiling water for 5 minutes.

Remove the tea pouch and allow the concentrate to cool to room temperature.

Add in your choice of sliced fruit and place the container in the fridge. Allow it to steep there for 6 hours.

When you are ready to serve, remove your container from the refrigerator and pour the sangria in a large pitcher over ice.

JASMINE MOJITO

8 teaspoons Jasmine Reserve (from Art of Tea)

4 cups boiling water

1 cup granulated sugar

½ cup hot water

1 cup ice

Juice of 2 limes

6 sprigs mint

3 cups club soda

Brew the Jasmine Reserve in the boiling water for 3 minutes, then strain the leaves. Allow the concentrate to cool to room temperature.

Dissolve the sugar into the cup of hot water to make a simple syrup. Then add the simple syrup, ice, and lime juice to a large pitcher. Add the mint leaves to the pitcher and muddle, and then the tea concentrate and club soda.

Stir and serve.

CREAMY APPLE CIDER

2 tablespoons Apple Pie Tea (Seasonal from Art of Tea)

8 ounces boiling water

2 cup whole or cashew milk

2 cinnamon sticks, broken or chopped

1 teaspoon ground cinnamon

1 tablespoon raw apple cider vinegar

1 red apple, chopped

Raw honey, to taste

Steep the Apple Pie Tea in the boiling water for 5–7 minutes.

In a saucepan over low-medium heat, bring the milk, cinnamon sticks, cinnamon, apple cider vinegar, and apple to a simmer.

Remove the cinnamon sticks and apple from the saucepan and pour the remaining liquid into the steeped Apple Pie Tea.

If you wish, sweeten the tea with honey. Enjoy!

BLOODY ORANGE CIDER

3 teaspoons Italian Blood Orange Tea (from Art of Tea)
16 ounces boiling water
1 ½ cups apple juice
¼ cup orange peel, zested
3 pinches cinnamon
Cinnamon sticks, to garnish

Steep the Italian Blood Orange tea in the boiling water for 5–7 minutes. Remove the leaves.

Add in the apple juice, sprinkle the orange peel, and sprinkle in the cinnamon.

For an extra kick of cinnamon, add a cinnamon stick to garnish.

ICED GREEN GIN TEA

1 teaspoon green tea or Liquid Jade Tea (from Art of Tea)

8 ounces boiling water

1 teaspoon honey, to taste

1 ½ ounces dry gin

Brew the green tea and let it steep for 3–5 minutes. Add the honey, then place the tea in the refrigerator to chill for 20 minutes.

Remove the tea from the refrigerator, add gin and ice, and serve!

ICED BOURBON PEACH TEA

1 teaspoon Summer Peach Tea (from Art of Tea)

8 ounces boiling water

1 teaspoon honey, to taste

1 ½ ounces bourbon

Slice of orange, to garnish

Brew the Summer Peach Tea for 3–5 minutes. Add the honey, then place the tea in the refrigerator to chill for 20 minutes.

Remove the tea from the refrigerator and add bourbon and ice. Garnish with the slice of orange and serve!

MINT GREEN MOJITO

1 teaspoon or 1 sachet of Moroccan Mint Tea (from Art of Tea)

8 ounces boiling water

½ lime, cut into wedges

10 mint sprigs

4 sugar cubes or 2 teaspoons sweetener of choice

1 ½ ounces light rum

Splash of soda water

Steep the Moroccan Mint tea in boiling water, and let it steep for 3–5 minutes. Allow the tea to cool to room temperature.

In a separate glass, muddle the lime wedges, mint sprigs, and sugar cubes. Add ice to the muddled mixture, then pour the rum and ½ cup of the tea into the glass and stir well. Top off the drink with a splash of soda.

Garnish with a slice of lime and mint sprig to serve.

MATCHA MELONBALL

½ teaspoon grade A matcha or 1 Matchastick from Art of Tea

½ ounce white crème de cacao

½ ounce triple sec

½ ounce vodka

Splash of coconut milk

Chill a martini glass to prepare.

Fill a cocktail shaker with ice and add in the matcha, white crème de cacao, triple sec, vodka, and coconut milk. Shake well.

Strain the mixture into the chilled martini glass.

BLOOD ORANGE BLISS

1 tablespoon or 1 sachet of Italian Blood Orange tea (from Art of Tea)

8 ounces boiling water

1 teaspoon orgeat syrup

1 ½ ounces vodka

½ ounce triple sec

Dash of orange bitters

1 ounce blood orange San Pellegrino

1 cinnamon stick, optional, for garnish

Steep the tea in the boiling water for 7 minutes. Fill a glass with ice and strain the tea into the chilled martini glass to flash-chill it.

In a cocktail shaker filled with ice, combine the orgeat syrup, vodka, triple sec, orange bitters, and blood orange San Pellegrino. Shake and pour into the chilled martini glass with the tea.

Garnish with cinnamon to serve.

TURMERIC GINGER CIDER

2 ½ tablespoons Bright Eyed tea (from Art of Tea)

16 ounces boiling water

6 ounces milk or milk substitute

2 ounces bourbon

1 ounce amaretto

2 cinnamon sticks, optional, for garnish

Steep the Bright Eyed tea in boiling water for 4 minutes, then allow it to cool to room temperature.

After the tea has cooled, pour it into a 24-ounce pitcher filled halfway with ice. Pour in the milk, bourbon, and amaretto. Stir well and pour the drink between 2 cocktail glasses. Garnish with cinnamon sticks if desired.

EARL GREY CRÉME OLD FASHIONED

1 teaspoon or 1 sachet Earl Grey Crème Tea (from Art of Tea)

8 ounces boiling water

3 maraschino cherries, plus 1 to garnish, if desired

1 sugar cube

1 orange peel

2 dashes Fee Brothers Old-Fashioned Bitters

1 ounce Whiskey

Splash of soda water

Orange slice, optional, to garnish

Steep the Earl Grey Crème Tea in boiling water for 3 minutes. Allow it to cool to room temperature.

In a rocks glass, muddle together the cherries, sugar cube, orange peel, and bitters. Add ice to the glass, and then pour 2 ounces of the Earl Grey Crème and the whiskey over the ice. Stir and finish the drink off with a splash of soda water.

Garnish with a cherry or slice of orange to serve.

FRENCH LEMON DROP

1 teaspoon or 1 sachet of French Lemon Ginger blend (from Art of Tea)

8 ounces boiling water

1 ½ ounces Absolut Citron

¼ ounce Cointreau

¼ ounce simple syrup

Sugar, optional, to rim glass

Lemon twist, optional, to garnish

Steep the French Lemon Ginger tea for 5–7 minutes. Allow it to cool to room temperature.

In a cocktail shaker filled with ice, combine the tea, Absolut Citron, Cointreau, and simple syrup. Shake well and strain the drink into a sugar-rimmed martini glass. Garnish with a lemon twist and serve.

THAT'S AMORÉ

1 tablespoon Tuscany Tea (from Art of Tea)

8 ounces boiling water

1 ½ ounces cucumber vodka

1 teaspoon simple syrup

Splash of lime juice

4–5 dashes rose water

Lime wedge, optional, to garnish

Cucumber wheel, optional, to garnish

Steep the Tuscany tea in the boiling water for 3 minutes. Allow it to cool to room temperature.

In a cocktail shaker filled with ice, combine 4 ounces of the tea with the cucumber vodka, simple syrup, lime juice, and rose water. Shake and strain the drink into a martini glass.

Garnish with a lime wedge or cucumber wheel to serve.

WELCOME TO BOURBON STREET

1 tablespoon Lavender Chamomile Rose Blend (from Art of Tea)

6 ounces boiling water

2 ounces whiskey

¼ ounce orange flower water

¼ ounce lavender syrup

Orange peel, to garnish

Steep the Lavender Chamomile Rose Blend in the boiling water for 5–7 minutes. Allow it to cool to room temperature.

In a rocks glass filled with ice, combine 3 ounces of the tea with the whiskey, orange flower water, and lavender syrup. Stir.

Garnish with an orange peel to serve. Makes 2 servings.

6:00 P.M. KICKOFF COCKTAIL

1 tablespoon London Tea (from Art of Tea)

3 ounces boiling water

2 ounces whiskey

¼ ounce orange flower water

¼ ounce lavender syrup

Orange peel, to garnish

Steep the London Tea in the boiling water for 5–7 minutes, then allow it to cool to room temperature.

In a rocks glass filled with ice, combine the cooled tea, whiskey, orange flower water, and lavender syrup. Stir and add an orange peel to garnish.

HOT TODDY

1 tablespoon of Egyptian Chamomile (from Art of Tea)

8 ounces boiling water

Honey, to taste

1 ½ ounce bourbon

Slice of orange, to garnish

Brew the Egyptian Chamomile for 3–5 minutes. Add the honey and bourbon. Garnish with orange to serve.

TEA TREATS AND DESSERTS

EARL GREY SHORTBREAD COOKIE RECIPE
From Katie Kirby

2 tablespoons loose-leaf Earl Grey tea, ground with a mortar and pestle or in a food processor

¾ cup powdered sugar

1 cup butter, room temperature

A few drops vanilla essence or extract

2 cups all-purpose flour

¼ teaspoon salt

2–3 ounces milk or dark chocolate, depending upon your preference

Line a food storage container with parchment paper.

In a large bowl, stir together the tea and powdered sugar until they are well incorporated. Add in the butter and blend or pulse them with the tea and sugar for approximately 3 minutes.

Add the vanilla, flour, and salt. Mix until they are just combined, taking care not to overmix.

Remove the dough to a clean, lightly floured surface. Roll the dough out to ¼-inch thickness. Using a heart-shaped cutter, cut out as many hearts as possible. Place them in the storage container; if necessary, create multiple layers in the container divided by parchment paper. Roll the leftover dough and continue cutting out hearts until you've used all of the dough. Seal the container and chill the cookies for at least 4 hours or up to a few days.

To bake the cookies, preheat the oven to 375 degrees and line a cookie sheet with parchment paper or a silicone baking sheet.

Bake the cookies for 13–15 minutes and allow them to cool completely before decorating.

Place the chocolate in a small saucepan over low heat until melted, stirring constantly. When the chocolate is melted, dip half of each cookie into the chocolate. Place the cookie on the parchment paper until the chocolate cools and hardens. If you want to cool the cookies more quickly, you can place them in the freezer for a few minutes.

The cookies can be stored in an airtight container for up to 1 week.

MEYER LEMON AND ROSE PETAL SHORTBREAD COOKIES

⅓ cup unsalted butter, room temperature

½ cup, plus 2 tablespoons raw cane sugar

½ teaspoon coarse salt

1 ½ tablespoons Meyer Lemon Tea (from Art of Tea), ground with a mortar and pestle or in a food processor so tea is broken down slightly

1 ½ tablespoons dried rose petals

½ teaspoon vanilla extract

2 cups all-purpose flour

Use a mixer to whip the butter. Add in the sugar and salt and mix a bit more, just enough that the ingredients are evenly combined. Mix in the tea, rose petals, and vanilla.

On low speed, incorporate the flour in ¼-cup increments. Continue mixing (without overmixing) until the dough is crumbly but uniform.

Form the dough into a flat disk and wrap it in plastic or place it between two sheets of parchment paper. Place it in the refrigerator to chill for 2 hours.

Roll the dough out on a lightly floured surface and roll to ½-inch thickness. Place the dough between two pieces of parchment paper and place it in the freezer for at least 30 minutes.

Remove the sheet of dough from the refrigerator and preheat the oven to 325 degrees. Line a baking tray with parchment paper.

Moving quickly so that the dough stays manageable, cut the cookies with your favorite cookie cutter and place them on the baking sheet. (If the dough begins to get too soft, return it to the freezer for 10 minutes.)

Bake the cookies for 15 minutes, then rotate the cookie sheet and bake them for an additional 10 minutes or until the cookies are golden brown.

Allow the cookies to cool on the baking sheet, and enjoy them with a cup of hot tea!

PUMPKIN CHAI CHEESECAKE TARTLETS

⅓ cup unsalted butter, softened

8 ounces cream cheese, softened

¾ cup sugar, plus ⅓ cup sugar, divided

5 large eggs

1 tablespoon vanilla extract

½ teaspoon cinnamon, plus ⅛ teaspoon, divided

3 tablespoons cornstarch

15-ounce canned pumpkin puree and tartlet shells

⅓ cup light brown sugar, packed

Pinch of cloves

Pinch of cardamom

Pinch of ginger

Pinch of nutmeg or ¾ teaspoon pumpkin pie blend (Seasonal at Art of Tea)

¼ teaspoon salt

¼ cup chai tea, strongly steeped (we recommend Art of Tea's Tali's Masala Chai)

½ cup heavy cream

Preheat the oven to 350 degrees.

In a medium-sized bowl, whip the butter with an electric mixer. Add the cream cheese and continue mixing. Add the sugar and beat until fluffy. Beat in 3 eggs, vanilla, ½ teaspoon cinnamon, and cornstarch.

Spray a small pan with cooking spray. Spoon a layer of the cream cheese mixture into tartlet shells so that they are no more than half full and place them onto the pan. Then place the smaller pan into a larger pan and fill the larger pan with water to create a 2-inch bath around the smaller pan. This will allow the heat to distribute evenly around the pan to prevent the cheesecake layer from cracking.

Place the pan in the oven and bake for 25 minutes.

While the cheesecake layer is baking, make the pumpkin layer. In a medium-sized bowl, mix the pumpkin puree and 2 eggs until they are well blended. Add in ⅓ cup sugar and the brown sugar and mix until smooth. Add in the additional cinnamon, cloves, cardamom, ginger, and nutmeg and mix until well blended.

Once the cheesecake layer has finished baking, pour the pumpkin layer over the cream cheese layer and bake another 30 minutes following the same directions with the baking pans. Allow the tartlets to cool to room temperature in the pan; then refrigerate and serve cold.

PUMPKIN CHAI CUPCAKES

7 tablespoons flour

½ teaspoon baking powder

⅛ teaspoon baking soda

¼ teaspoon salt

½ teaspoon cinnamon

¼ teaspoon ground ginger

¼ teaspoon nutmeg, freshly grated

1 large egg

½ cup pumpkin puree

¼ cup brown sugar

3 tablespoons sugar

3 tablespoons vegetable oil

1 teaspoon of Pumpkin Spice Chai (Seasonal from Art of Tea)

1 ⅓ cups powdered sugar

¼ cup butter, softened

Preheat the oven to 350 degrees.

Prepare a muffin pan with 4 cupcake liners.

In a small bowl, whisk together the flour, baking powder, baking soda, salt, cinnamon, ginger, and nutmeg.

In a medium bowl, whisk together the egg, pumpkin puree, brown sugar, sugar, and vegetable oil.

Add together the wet and dry mixture and stir them together without overmixing.

Divide the batter evenly between the cupcake liners and bake for 28–32 minutes, or until a toothpick inserted comes out clean.

While the cupcakes cool, begin preparing the frosting by pouring boiling water over the Pumpkin Spice Chai bag and allowing it to steep for 10 minutes. As it steeps, beat together the butter and powdered sugar until fluffy; this should take between 3 and 4 minutes. Add two tablespoons of the brewed tea and mix well.

When the cupcakes have cooled completely, frost them and serve.

MATCHA GREEN TEA PROTEIN TRUFFLES

1 scoop chocolate protein powder

1 cup almond butter

1 cup almonds, crushed

½ teaspoon grade A matcha or 1 Matchastick from Art of Tea, plus extra matcha to coat the truffles

1 ½ teaspoons agave or honey (optional)

1 teaspoon unsweetened cocoa powder

½ teaspoon cinnamon, plus extra to coat the truffles

Cover the bottom of a freezer-friendly storage container with parchment paper.

In a large bowl, thoroughly mix together the protein powder, almond butter, almonds, matcha, and agave (if desired) until the color is an even dark chocolate hue.

Mix together the cocoa powder and cinnamon in a small bowl.

Use a melon baller to create equally portioned truffles. Dust your hands with the cocoa powder and cinnamon mixture as you ball the truffles. Place each truffle into the storage container. Once they are placed, sprinkle a little matcha and cinnamon over each truffle.

Cover the storage container and place it into the freezer for 2 hours.

Enjoy a protein-packed truffle before and after your next workout! Store in the freezer and allow 15–30 minutes to thaw before consuming, based on your preference.

MATCHA CUPCAKES

1 cup unsalted butter, room temperature

2 cups sugar

2 large eggs

2 large egg yolks

3 cups all-purpose flour

2 teaspoons baking powder

⅛ teaspoon salt

1 cup milk

3 tablespoons grade A matcha

1 sixteen-ounce tub cream cheese frosting

Preheat the oven to 350 degrees.

Prepare a muffin pan with cupcake liners.

Using a mixer or blender, beat the butter until it's soft. Add in the sugar and whip for a couple of minutes more, until the mixture is light and fluffy. Add the eggs and egg yolks, one at a time, making sure to combine each one into the mixture fully before adding in the next.

In a separate bowl, whisk together the flour, baking powder, and salt. Add the dry mixture to the batter and mix to combine.

In a separate bowl, whisk together the milk and the matcha. Then add the mixture to the batter.

Spoon the batter into the cupcake liner, filling each one two-thirds full. Place the tray in the oven and bake for approximately 22 minutes or until a toothpick comes out clean.

Allow the cupcakes to cool on a wire cooling rack before frosting with the cream cheese frosting.

MATCHA POUND CAKE

½ cup butter, room temperature

1 cup sugar

2 eggs

½ cup milk

3 drops vanilla extract

1 cup all-purpose flour

2 tablespoons matcha

1 teaspoon baking powder

¼ teaspoon salt

Preheat the oven to 325 degrees.

Line a loaf pan with parchment paper or grease it with butter, then dust it evenly with flour.

In a mixer, add the butter and sugar, and cream them together. Add the eggs, milk, and vanilla extract and beat until well combined.

In a separate bowl, mix together the flour, matcha, baking powder, and salt. Slowly add the dry mixture to the wet mixture and blend them together until they are smooth.

Pour the batter into the prepared loaf pan. Bake for approximately 45 minutes, or until the cake is golden.

Remove the loaf from the oven and allow it to sit for 10 minutes before removing it from the pan to cool completely on a wire rack.

CHOCOLATE MATCHA TRUFFLES

8 ounces (about 1 ⅓ cup) white chocolate, finely chopped

¼ cup unsalted butter

⅓ cup heavy cream

Pinch of salt

2 ½ teaspoons grade A matcha

1 teaspoon powdered sugar

1 ten-ounce bag dark chocolate chips

1 teaspoon coconut oil

Place the white chocolate into a ceramic or heat-friendly bowl and set it aside.

Add the butter and cream to a saucepan and heat it over low heat. Add the salt and approximately half of the matcha. Keep the mixture over the heat and stir occasionally, until it starts to bubble and the matcha is fully blended in.

Pour the hot cream mixture over the chocolate and mix until the chocolate is completely melted and the mixture is smooth. Cover and place the bowl in the refrigerator and allow it to chill overnight.

After the mixture has chilled, line a plate or tray with parchment paper.

Mix the remaining matcha and powdered sugar into a small bowl.

Place the dark chocolate chips and coconut oil in a micro-wave-safe bowl. Microwave for approximately 3–4 thirty-second intervals, stirring often. Once the chocolate is melted, remove the white chocolate mixture from the fridge.

Using a spoon, scoop and shape the chilled white chocolate mixture into balls. Coat each ball with melted dark chocolate, and sprinkle the matcha and powdered sugar mixture on top. Place each completed truffle on the parchment-lined plate or tray.

Place the truffles into the freezer for approximately an hour, until they are firm. Extras can be stored in an airtight container in the fridge.

EARL GREY CHOCOLATE CAKE

¾ cup butter

6 teaspoons Earl Grey tea, ground into a fine powder using a mortar and pestle

1 ¼ all-purpose flour

¼ cup unsweetened cocoa powder

1 ½ teaspoons baking soda

2 ½ teaspoons baking powder

1 ½ cups brown sugar, packed

½ teaspoon salt

3 eggs

2 cups buttermilk

6 ounces semisweet chocolate chips

1 tablespoon sugar

4 ounces heavy cream

8 ounces cream cheese

8 ounces powdered sugar, sifted

1 teaspoon vanilla extract

Preheat the oven to 325 degrees.

Grease two 9-inch cake pans with butter and dust with flour to ensure even coverage.

Melt 1 stick of butter in a small saucepan over low heat. Add the Earl Grey powder and cook for 10 minutes, stirring occasionally until the tea flavor has infused into the butter. Remove the butter from the heat and allow it to cool for 10 minutes.

While the butter is cooling, sift the flour, cocoa powder, baking soda, and baking powder into a large mixing bowl. Add the brown sugar and salt, then whisk to combine. In a separate bowl, beat together the eggs and buttermilk until combined.

Once the tea butter has cooled, add it to the dry mixture. Then add the buttermilk mixture and beat until the ingredients are just combined. It's okay if the batter is slightly lumpy, and it's important not to overwork the batter so that the cake will be light and fluffy.

Divide the batter evenly between the 2 cake pans and bake for 30–35 minutes. Remove the cake pans from the oven and allow them to sit for at least 10 minutes before removing the cakes from the pans and placing them on a wire cooling rack. Allow them to cool on the rack for about 1 hour.

As the cake is cooling, you can begin to make the chocolate ganache. Place the chocolate chips and sugar in a heat-proof bowl and set it aside. In a saucepan, heat the heavy cream over medium heat until it begins to simmer. Pour the heavy cream over the chocolate-sugar mixture and allow it to sit for 1 minute, then whisk until all of the chocolate melts and the mixture is smooth. Set the mixture aside for 20 minutes to allow it to cool before spreading on the cake.

To prepare the cream cheese frosting, place the cream cheese, ½ stick of butter, powdered sugar, and vanilla extract into a large bowl and beat until completely smooth.

Once the cake has cooled, place a plate on top of one of the cakes and flip it over. Spread the chocolate ganache over the top of the first layer of cake. Place the second layer of cake on top of the first. Use a spatula to spread the cream cheese frosting over the entire cake.

CHAI ROOT BEER FLOAT

2 teaspoons Tali's Masala Chai (from Art of Tea)

8 ounces hot water (195°F)

4 ounces root beer

2 scoops vanilla ice cream

Place a root beer mug in the freezer to chill.

Steep Tali's Masala Chai in the hot water, allowing it to steep for 10 minutes.

Place the tea in the refrigerator for approximately 2 hours to allow it to chill.

Combine the chai concentrate and root beer into the chilled mug. Scoop in the ice cream and enjoy!

GREEN TEA ICE CREAM

1 pint vanilla ice cream
1 teaspoon grade A matcha or 2 Art of Tea Matchasticks
Blueberries (optional)

Place the ice cream in a bowl. Sprinkle the matcha over the ice cream. (We recommend 1 teaspoon of matcha per pint of ice cream, but adjust the ratio to your taste.)

Use a spoon to incorporate the matcha into the ice cream, mixing well.

To serve, garnish with blueberries or the toppings of your choice.

To refreeze the ice cream, simply cover the bowl with plastic wrap and place the bowl in the freezer.

WHITE COCONUT CRÈME TEA POPS

8 ounces White Coconut Crème Tea (from Art of Tea)

8 ounces coconut cream

Cold-brew the White Coconut Crème Tea for 8 to 12 hours (see Chapter Seven for cold brew instructions)

Note that these popsicles will consist of alternating layers of White Coconut Creme Tea and coconut creme. You can determine how thick each of these layers is, depending upon your preference and the size of your popsicle mold.

Begin by pouring a layer of coconut cream into your popsicle mold, and freeze for approximately 1 hour. Remove the popsicle mold from the freezer and add a layer of the brewed tea over the coconut cream. Freeze for 1 more hour.

Continue alternating the layers as desired, allowing each layer to freeze for 1 hour before adding the next. Once you have filled the mold, allow the popsicles to freeze for 24 hours before enjoying.

ACKNOWLEDGMENTS

Thank you to Don Riddell, who has taught me so much about what it means to be a thoughtful leader. *"What stories did I believe today that didn't serve me well? Those stories only have power to the extent that they give me power."*

Special thanks to my wife and kids for allowing me the space and opportunity to focus on this writing project to further expand the vision of Art of Tea.

Thank you to the talented and growing team at Art of Tea. This book is for you and the future generations at Art of Tea to help continue to lead the way beyond my time on this planet.

Thank you to Nikki Van Noy for tracking with me on this book. Countless revisions and thoughtful conversations helped bring past and present learnings to our tribe. Bringing this book to life would not have been possible without your writing talent.

Thank you to David Robins, Chef Lee, Chef Ari, and Laura McIver for believing in me and our wonderful tea so early on. This gave Art of Tea a starting point that we could not have had without you.

Thank you to Diana Hossfeld for helping to express written details on the book and share the message with the world.

Thank you to the Scribe Team for their guidance on how to best bring this book to life.

Thank you to my brother and sister, who relentlessly believed in me from a young age when our parents were nowhere to be seen. Your belief in me helped frame the person I continually want to become.

To our Art of Tea tribe, thank you for continuing to bring our community closer together and enriching lives everyday through the timeless art and ritual of tea.

ABOUT THE AUTHOR

S teve Schwartz, founder of Art of Tea, is a master tea blender, international keynote speaker, loving husband, and father to three girls. With a background in Ayurveda from the Ayurvedic Institute in New Mexico, Steve crafts award-winning teas that showcase his passion for the alchemy of blending.

Steve has traveled the globe to cultivate long-lasting relationships with farmers and source the highest quality of ingredients. He and his company have been featured in *O*, *Forbes*, *HuffPost*, and the *Los Angeles Times*. Steve is a globally recognized leader for building an impact-driven culture through tea. Connect with him at Artoftea.com/book.

CPSIA information can be obtained
at www.ICGtesting.com
Printed in the USA
BVHW090241281122
652699BV00001B/1/J